PRAISE FOR
FOLLOW THE EVIDENCE

"These days, science and faith often feel like they're at odds—but *Follow the Evidence* offers a fresh, thoughtful perspective. Bruce Cook invites readers to explore some of life's biggest questions with both reason and belief in mind. This book speaks to skeptics, challenges the curious, and encourages believers—all through a compelling story that makes tough ideas easy to understand."

SONNY PERDUE, Chancellor of the University System of Georgia, former Governor of Georgia, 31st United States Secretary of Agriculture

"This is a book that needed to be written. I can relate to it personally, having been a skeptic myself until age thirty-two. Few books clearly present the scientific evidence for a God who is active in our daily lives—but Bruce Cook, a man of deep faith, integrity, and intellect, has done just that. In a engaging way, he lays out the scientific indicators that point unmistakably to God. I recommend it to anyone wrestling with doubts or seeking encouragement that faith and science are not at odds. My hope is that millions will read it and discover the compelling case this book makes."

RON BLUE, Founder of the Ronald Blue Company, Best-Selling Author and Speaker

"In *Follow the Evidence*, Bruce Cook tackles one of humanity's most enduring questions: *How did we get here, and where are we going?* Bruce hits a 'home run' in creating a dialogue between two protagonists who meet on a cruise and engage with expert-led lectures to deliver a narrative that is both engaging and intellectually stimulating. A must-read for anyone wrestling with the deeper questions of existence and the intersection of science and faith."

PHIL GINGREY, MD, former US Congressman

"Bruce Cook's *Follow the Evidence* is a clear, concise, and compelling resource that distills the growing scientific and historic evidence for a theistic worldview. His engaging use of a personal dialogue on a cruise ship makes it winsome and accessible, and this will serve many as an effective and nonthreatening evangelistic tool."

| Dr. KENNETH BOA, Reflections Ministries

"My friend Bruce Cook has given to us a wonderful resource, presenting the evidence for the existence of God in a creative, warm, and inviting way. This book is written with such winsome clarity, appealing to both the mind and the heart. Thank you, Bruce, for giving us such a compelling, timely resource that will not only encourage and equip us in sharing the love and hope of Christ but also [serve as] a gift we can pass on."

| Dr. CRAWFORD W. LORITTS Jr., Founder and President of
Beyond Our Generation, Author, Speaker

"If you've ever wondered, 'What—or Who—created our universe? Is there really a God? Is there life after death? Was Jesus who He claimed to be? Is the Bible a reliable historical account or just a myth?'—then you need to read *Follow the Evidence*. Bruce Cook has distilled clear, compelling answers to these and other life-shaping questions, offering insights that can lead to a more purposeful and joyful life."

| STEVE FRANKLIN, PhD, former Associate Dean of
Emory University Goizueta Business School

"I have walked with God and served in ministry for more than sixty years. On rare occasions, life events—world and personal—sneak in to suggest doubts about the validity of my faith. But Bruce has given me all the evidence I need to resist them and to live confidently in the truths God has given. Not a dry academic book, but a captivating story of discovery. Thank you, Bruce!!"

| JUDY DOUGLASS, Global Director of Cru Women's Resources,
Author, Speaker

FOLLOW THE
EVIDENCE

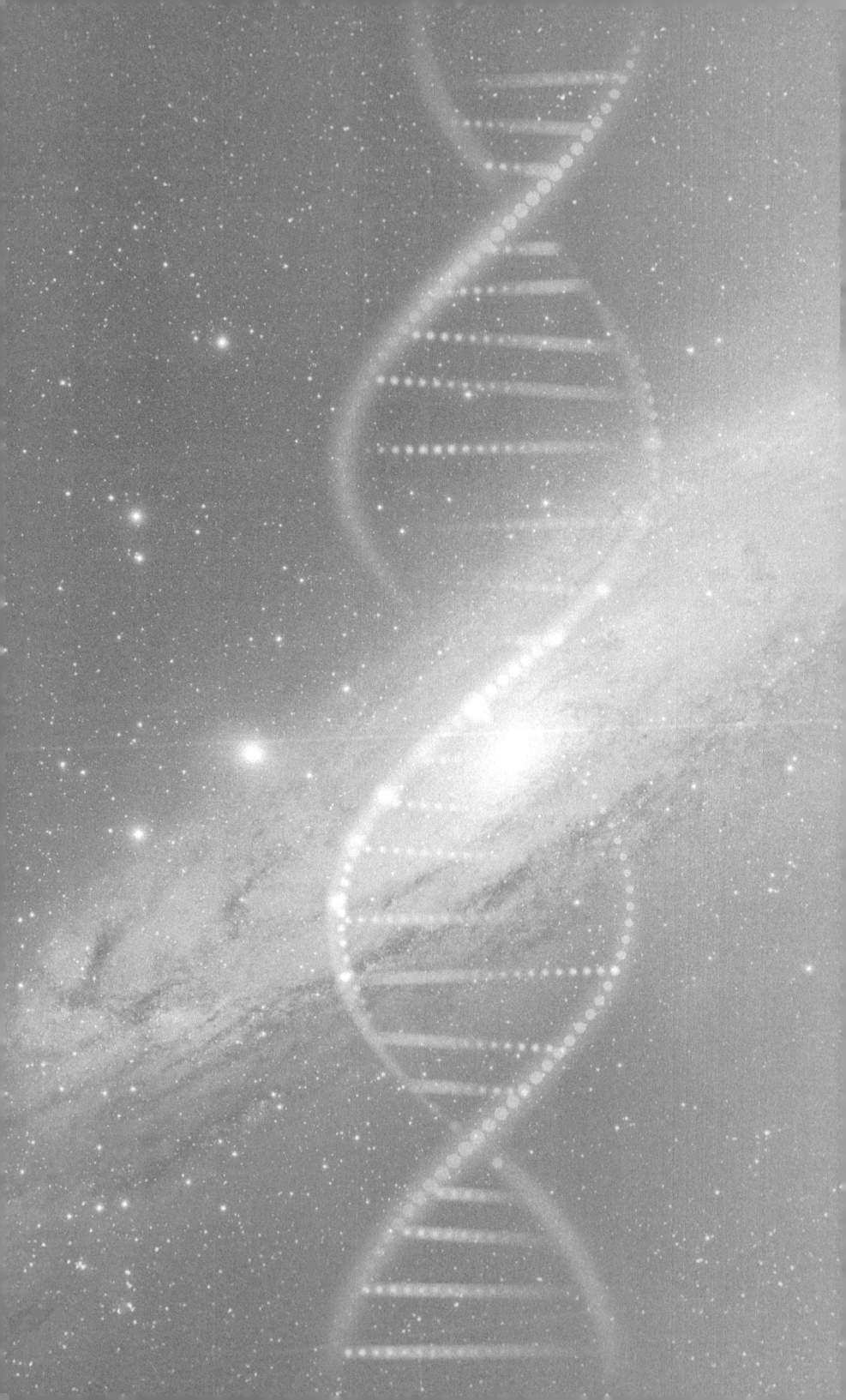

FOLLOW THE EVIDENCE

WHAT SCIENCE REVEALS ABOUT THE EXISTENCE OF GOD

BRUCE COOK

FOLLOW THE EVIDENCE
What Science Reveals About the Existence of God

Copyright © 2025 by Bruce Cook

Disclaimer: This book has been published for the purpose of providing the reader with general information on its subject matter. The author and the publisher believe the information to be accurate and authoritative at the time of publication. The book is sold with the understanding that neither the author nor the publisher is providing professional advice, and the reader should not rely upon this book as such. Every situation is different, and professional advice (whether psychological, legal, financial, tax, or otherwise) should only be obtained from a professional licensed in your jurisdiction who has knowledge of the specific facts and circumstances.

All scripture quotations, unless otherwise marked, are taken from the New International Version.

Interior Layout and Design by Stephanie Anderson
Book Cover Design by Suzanna Chriscoe
Editorial Team: Teresa Miller, Marcie Taylor, Kiska Carr

ISBNs:
979-8-89165-312-2 *Paperback*
979-8-89165-311-5 *Hardback*
979-8-89165-313-9 *E-book*

Published by:
Streamline Books
Kansas City, MO
shareyourstory.com

To "Alex," whom I met on a cruise—
and whose conversation inspired this book

CONTENTS

ACKNOWLEDGMENTS |

I am deeply grateful to several people who played a vital role in bringing *Follow the Evidence* to life.

First, my heartfelt thanks to my good friend Charlie Paparelli. It was Charlie's initial encouragement that sparked the idea of writing a nonfiction book in a fictional format. His investment of time—reading multiple drafts and providing strategic, reader-focused feedback—was instrumental in shaping the book. Charlie's relentless pursuit of clarity and impact kept the manuscript sharply aligned with its intended audience, and for that, I am truly thankful.

I'm also deeply appreciative of Pat MacMillan, another trusted friend, who patiently walked through chapter after chapter with me. His thoughtful critiques helped ensure that the dialogue between Alex and Sam remained authentic, engaging, and believable.

Thanks as well to Gregg Hinthorn for his expert guidance in refining the manuscript's structure. His contributions were key to building a narrative flow that would hold the reader's attention from beginning to end.

A special thanks to Annika Campbell for her keen editorial eye and skillful editing. Her thoughtful input and attention to clarity, tone, and flow helped make this a better and more enjoyable read.

Finally, and most importantly, I want to thank my wife, Donna. Her steady encouragement—often summed up in the simple words, "hang in there" and "just get it done"—gave me the strength to finish. Her patience, support, and belief in this project have been a true gift.

To each of you—my deepest thanks.

INTRODUCTION |

The idea for this book began on a cruise.

My wife and I were traveling with friends when I discovered one of the featured speakers during our days at sea was a well-known national TV personality and political commentator. He was intelligent, accomplished, and constantly surrounded by admirers hoping for a photo or a moment of conversation.

I invited him to join me in the lounge for drinks before dinner. I was determined to stay away from politics and asked questions about his personal life and background. We discovered we were the same age and shared similar backgrounds of having limited financial resources and working our way through college.

When he asked what I had done after graduating from Georgia Tech and Harvard Business School, it opened the door for me to share my story of how as an agnostic I came to faith in Christ and ultimately joined the staff of a Christian organization. The conversation soon shifted to deeper topics: spiritual beliefs, the existence of God, Jesus, the Bible.

He was thoughtful, honest, and clearly skeptical. He was an atheist and his questions were real: *Is there any actual evidence for God? Was Jesus even a historical figure? Isn't the Bible just a man-made book full of contradictions?*

As we wrapped up, I asked him if he'd be open to reading a book that might speak to some of those questions. He said yes—*but keep it short.*

Coming home after the cruise, I searched for a book that could do just that. I needed something clear, engaging, and concise—approachable enough not to overwhelm, yet substantial enough to answer his deepest questions. Something that respected skepticism but didn't shy away from serious evidence. Something concise enough to hold his attention—but meaningful enough to engage his most serious doubts.

I couldn't find it.

So, I wrote it.

FOLLOW THE EVIDENCE centers on two fictional characters, Sam and Alex—friends from their college days who unexpectedly reconnect on a cruise sponsored by the Faith-Science Alliance.

Alex is an atheist who believes that life's biggest questions are best answered by science alone. Sam, on the other hand, believes in God and sees science not as a threat to faith, but as pointing toward the existence of a creator.

During the cruise, the two attend a series of thought-provoking lectures by leading scientists and professors on topics at the intersection of faith and science: the laws of nature, the origin of the universe, the design of DNA, the enigma of consciousness, and more.

Together, Sam and Alex wrestle with a fundamental question: **Does science explain away the need for God, or does it uncover evidence for his existence?**

FOLLOW THE EVIDENCE isn't just Sam and Alex's story. It's a reflection of the conversations many of us have—sometimes quietly within ourselves—about what's true and why it matters. As you read, I invite you to ask the hard questions and to follow the evidence wherever it leads.

—BRUCE COOK

CHAPTER 1

The Journey Begins

T HE SUN DIPPED low on the horizon, casting a golden hue over the endless ocean as the cruise ship swayed gently in the evening breeze. Sam leaned against the railing of the SS *Aurora*, a warm breeze ruffling his hair. He had come on the cruise not only to get a break from his hectic life as a project manager but also to explore a topic he had been interested in since college: the intersection of faith and science.

The cruise had been organized by The Faith and Science Alliance, a collaborative organization dedicated to bridging the gap between faith communities and the scientific community. Sam had heard the cruise would be packed with experts in fields like astronomy, biology, and psychology.

Suddenly, a familiar voice broke through the crowd: "Sam? Is that really you?"

Sam turned. Standing there, looking slightly disheveled but still familiar, was Alex, an old friend from college. In those days, they had often butted heads over religion versus science; Sam believed in God, and Alex did not.

The years had changed them both. Alex's once-bright eyes now had shadows of weariness, perhaps relating to the recent divorce he had mentioned in their last conversation together.

"Alex! I can't believe you're here!" Sam exclaimed, giving his friend a warm embrace. "Who knew *you'd* be interested in anything dealing with faith and science?"

"Well," Alex replied, forcing a smile that didn't quite reach his eyes, "I'm just here for a mental break, you know? Work's been overwhelming, and I figured a cruise would help me unwind."

"As for this particular cruise," Alex added, giving a tired chuckle, "I got a good deal from *Scientific Nature*, the magazine I'm working for, to come on the cruise and write an article about my experiences. In all honesty, I just needed a change of scenery. But of all the places to bump into you—a cruise hosted by a *faith-science* group, no less. That's some cosmic irony."

"Right? It's like God's got a sense of humor."

Alex grinned, "You *would* say that."

As they made their way to a quiet lounge on the deck, Sam and Alex reminisced about old times. They had first met in a packed lecture hall, where Sam's sincere questions about the origins of life had caught Alex's attention. Back in college, the two had shared countless conversations on the intersection of faith and science. Despite their opposing views—Sam's steady belief in God and Alex's probing skepticism—their discussions quickly evolved into spirited, thought-provoking debates that both of them came to value.

Alex asked, "Do you remember that time in Dr. Helms's philosophy of science class? We practically took over the discussion about the Big Bang."

Sam nodded. "You argued it was just a random quantum

event, and I kept saying, 'Everything that begins to exist has a cause.'"

Alex laughed. "And you kept quoting the Kalam cosmological argument like it was scripture."

"Guilty. But you have to admit that it does raise the question: If the universe had a beginning, doesn't that beg for the existence of a beginner?"

"Or . . . it just means we haven't found the natural explanation yet. Science doesn't need a supernatural placeholder every time we hit a wall."

"Sure," Sam responded, "but if everything material, space, and time came into existence at the Big Bang, doesn't the cause have to be *immaterial, timeless,* and *powerful?*"

Alex laughed. "And round and invisible too?"

"Remember that night in the dorm lounge when we stayed up until 3:00 a.m. arguing about morality?"

Alex exclaimed, "How could I forget?! You said if God doesn't exist, there's no objective right or wrong. I said morality is evolutionary—survival strategy, group cohesion, that sort of thing."

"Right," Sam countered, "And I said, if that's true, then the Holocaust isn't *really* evil—it's just evolution taking a dark turn."

"You always hit hard with that. Still think there's no basis for human rights without God?"

Folding his arms, Sam replied, "Still do. If we're just cosmic accidents, then there's no 'ought'—only preference. But if we're made in God's image, then every person has inherent value and dignity."

"Or maybe we just *want* that to be true. And how could I forget Easter weekend senior year—you tried to convince me the resurrection of Jesus was historically credible."

Sam grinned. "I brought out the big guns—empty tomb, eyewitnesses, changed lives."

"Yeah," Alex said, chuckling, "and I hit back with hallucinations, legends, and the idea that people die for causes all the time."

"True, but people don't knowingly die for what they know is a lie. The disciples believed they saw him alive—and their willingness to suffer for it is hard to explain away."

"I don't know," replied Alex. "I still think legends can grow fast in ancient cultures."

"Or maybe something actually happened that changed everything." Sam paused to remember and added, "Then there was that argument sophomore year in the quad—you said life can have meaning without God."

Alex nodded. "Right. I argued we create our own meaning. That we don't need a cosmic parent handing us a purpose. We make our own."

"And I said that's like writing poetry in the sand when the tide is coming in. If life is ultimately just matter in motion—atoms, time, and chance—then no matter how meaningful it feels, it all ends in silence. It's borrowed meaning."

Alex quickly replied, "And I fired back that meaning doesn't have to be eternal to be real. We make it matter while we're here."

"But I asked, 'What if there *is* a designer who made you with meaning built in? Wouldn't that be deeper than something we invent to distract ourselves?'"

Alex smiled. "You always had a way of making things heavier than I wanted them to be."

"Just trying to keep you honest."

"Back then," Alex reflected, "I thought I had the upper hand most of the time. Now . . . I'm not so sure."

"Perspectives do change with age and life experiences."

Alex swirled his coffee and said, "You know . . . I used to love those arguments. Even if we never landed in the same place, you always made me think."

"And you sharpened me more than you know. Iron sharpens iron, right?"

Alex laughed. "There you go again—quoting Proverbs like we're back in our comparative religion class."

Sam grinned. "Some things don't change."

"So," Alex asked, "still holding on to your belief in God?"

Sam sipped his drink. "I'd say yes. Haven't found a reason to let it go."

"I'm guessing you know my stance," Alex said drily. "I'm still a skeptic. Science can explain a lot of what goes on around us."

Sam gave him a friendly shrug. "Maybe not everything."

Before Alex could respond, an announcement crackled over the ship's loudspeaker, inviting passengers to a welcome reception for the cruise's lecture series. Scientists from different fields would be giving talks all week.

Alex stood, draining the last of his drink. "Let's see if any of these experts bring up God, or if it's all about cosmic dust."

Sam laughed. "You never know."

They joined the crowd heading inside, and Sam wondered if this strange reunion might lead to something more than just a few heated debates.

> QUESTION FOR REFLECTION: *To what degree does your worldview, either as a naturalist or someone who believes in God, shape your perspective on life?*

CHAPTER 2

Who Wrote the Laws?

MORNING BROKE WITH a dazzling glow over the horizon. Sam strolled the ship's promenade deck, coffee in hand, letting the breeze wake him fully. He spotted Alex leaning casually on the rail, scanning the list of daily seminars on his phone.

"Who knew you'd become a morning person?" Sam asked.

Alex smiled. "Everyone changes eventually. Ready for the first lecture? It's on 'The Laws of Nature.' Should be right up your alley."

Sam and Alex found the location for the lecture inside a medium-sized lounge, where about two dozen people sat facing a small stage. Sam paused at the threshold to admire the floor-to-ceiling windows revealing the glittering ocean beyond. Alex found two seats for them near the front and waved Alex over. Just then, a tall, bespectacled man walked to the front where a lectern stood with a microphone. He gently tapped the microphone to ensure it was live and then cleared his throat.

"Good morning," he said. "I'm Dr. Charles Morgan. Let's explore the building blocks of reality—those laws of nature we sometimes take for granted. In the vast expanse of the universe, an unbroken set of laws orchestrates an incredible symphony. These laws of nature form the underlying code that governs everything from the intricate dance of galaxies to the blossom of a flower.

"Often these laws of nature can be expressed in precise mathematical formulas that work 100 percent of the time and run through every thread of scientific inquiry. When we observe consistent patterns in how things work, like gravity making apples fall or planets orbiting stars, we describe these patterns as 'laws.' They're like the universe's built-in rules—discovered over time, always present, and governing everything. The origins of these laws are tied to the very existence and nature of the universe. Scientists strive to understand and describe these laws by studying the universe itself.

"Perhaps the most recognized, Newton's laws fundamentally transformed our understanding of movement. Newton's insights explain why a rocket launches into space (action and reaction) and how a football arcs perfectly when kicked (forces and motion). These laws settled our solar system's grand architecture, allowing precise calculations of planetary orbits.

"The laws of thermodynamics dictate how energy flows and transforms within any system, crucial for understanding life itself. The sunlight hitting Earth powers photosynthesis and cycles energy through ecosystems. The energy our bodies use comes from the food we consume measured in calories. The body converts this chemical energy stored in food into kinetic energy for movement and thermal energy for maintaining body temperature. The engines in cars work by converting fuel into kinetic energy to move the vehicle.

"Maxwell's equations united electricity, magnetism, and light into four unified equations. This theoretic elegance allows us to predict how electric fields and magnetic fields interact. These equations make our modern world possible, describing how radios work, how light travels, and they presaged the development of technologies that underpin our communication systems."

As Dr. Morgan continued, he identified and explained numerous other "laws of nature." Finally, he concluded, "Science reveals through these laws a universe of order and predictability, an idea that has philosophical resonance beyond the material world.

"While these laws tell us 'how,' they also prompt us to ask 'why?' Why is the universe comprehensible and governed by consistent principles we can decipher through mathematics?

"From a naturalist perspective, these laws emerged with the formation of the universe and are intrinsic to its structure. They aren't prescribed by an external force but are inherent rules that we discover through observation and experimentation.

"On the other hand, some argue these questions point toward a purposeful design, suggesting not random happenstance but intentionality. They see in the universe's laws the fingerprints of a creator—an architect who devised the cosmos from an elegant blueprint.

"Einstein marveled at these orderly rules, calling it astounding that the universe is comprehensible at all. He often spoke about his belief in a cosmic order that hinted at a higher power. Newton saw in gravity the hand of God holding the universe's foundational workings. Darwin wrote of the impossibility of conceiving the universe as a result of blind chance without looking to a first cause having an intelligent mind."

As Dr. Morgan spoke, Alex scribbled in a small notebook. Sam could guess what he was jotting down: probably bits of science that seemed to leave no room for the supernatural.

Then came the after-lecture mingle. Sam and Alex approached Dr. Morgan near the coffee table.

"Great talk," Sam said. "My friend Alex here would say these laws explain away the need for God. How would you respond to that?"

The professor looked at Alex thoughtfully and said, "Some argue these laws simply 'are.' Others suspect there's a deeper cause—perhaps a designer. It's ultimately a philosophical question. Science can describe how things operate, but not always why they exist."

Alex shrugged. "That's where I say we don't need an extra layer. Nature's enough."

Dr. Morgan's expression remained thoughtful, not dismissive. "Fair stance. As I mentioned in my talk, Einstein wasn't conventionally religious, yet he spoke of a profound mystery behind the cosmos. It doesn't force a belief in God, but it can invite us to wonder."

A faint spark of annoyance crossed Alex's face. "I guess I'm not that easily invited."

Dr. Morgan chuckled. "Well, keep exploring. That's what science—and maybe faith—is all about."

They exchanged polite nods, and then Alex and Sam drifted back to the deck. The ocean stretched around them, vast and unhurried. They leaned on the railing, silent for a few moments.

Alex broke the silence, hands in his pockets. "Well, that was a different kind of science lecture. I thought we were going to talk about physics—he ended up talking about purpose."

Sam smiled. "Yeah, Dr. Morgan has a way of sneaking philosophy into the back door of cosmology."

Alex turned towards Sam. "I have to admit, when he asked, 'Why does the universe have laws in the first place?'—that caught me off guard. I've asked a lot of questions, but I never really thought to ask that one."

Sam nodded. "Same here. We take the laws of nature for granted—gravity, electromagnetism, the speed of light—all beautifully ordered, consistent, mathematical. But why should the universe be that way? Why should anything be law-governed at all?"

Alex shrugged. "I don't know. I guess I just assume it *is* that way. Maybe the laws are just inherent to the fabric of the universe—like ripples in a pond. No one has to make them; they just are."

"But do we see that kind of order coming out of nowhere in any other area of life? Think about it: When we see a law, we usually assume a lawgiver. If the universe operates according to precise, intelligible laws, isn't it reasonable to ask whether there's a mind behind them?"

"Or maybe the laws are just emergent properties—like patterns that settle in as the universe unfolds. Natural selection gave rise to order in biology; maybe something like that happened at the cosmological level."

Sam countered, "But laws don't *evolve*. They're constants. From the very beginning, they had to be in place—or there wouldn't be a stable universe to evolve anything in. And they're not just chaotic rules—they're mathematical, elegant, and discoverable. Doesn't that suggest intelligence?"

Alex paused, clearly thinking. "Maybe . . . But that's a big leap. Couldn't intelligence be something we're projecting onto the universe? We're pattern seekers by nature."

"Sure, but we don't project patterns that aren't there. The universe *is* ordered. The laws aren't just useful—they're the same laws that make stars burn, atoms bond, planets orbit, and brains think. It's not just that the universe is law-abiding—it's intelligible. That's what Einstein marveled at—not just that we can observe the universe, but that it makes *sense* to us."

"I'll give you this, Sam—it's hard to imagine something so finely tuned and orderly not having some kind of explanation. But why does that have to be God?"

"It doesn't have to be. But if the universe began to exist, and it's governed by consistent, knowable laws, and those laws seem tailor-made for life . . . then doesn't a rational, purposeful mind become a pretty strong candidate?"

Alex leaned back. "I'm not sure I can buy that totally. But I'll admit—it's harder to hold onto the idea that it all 'just happened' the more we learn about how it works."

Sam smiled. "Sometimes the questions are more important than the conclusions—especially when they won't leave you alone."

They continued walking slowly along the deck, the sea stretching out before them. The laws of the universe were still intact, as ever. But Sam had the feeling that inside Alex, something else was stirring—perhaps an unsettling thought that maybe, just maybe, there was an argument for a lawgiver behind it all.

> QUESTION FOR REFLECTION: *Since the laws of nature reflect predictability and order, does that very predictability become a sign of something—or someone—behind them?*

CHAPTER 3

In the Beginning

L ATER THAT EVENING, after a satisfying dinner in the ship's elegant dining hall, Sam and Alex strolled toward the bar on the aft deck. The space was lively yet inviting—a blend of polished wood, warm lighting, and a low murmur of conversation punctuated by occasional laughter and the clink of glasses. Unlike the hushed ambiance of the café earlier, the bar buzzed with a vibrant energy.

As they joined the steadily moving line to order drinks, the scent of citrus from garnishes mingled with the briny tang of sea air drifting in through open windows. Sam ordered a crisp lager that glinted golden in the low light, while Alex chose a robust dark ale. Amid the convivial bustle, a casually dressed man in a neatly pressed shirt caught their eye. His name tag read "Dr. Michael Guillen—Cosmology," and he was engaged in an animated conversation with the bartender about an upcoming sports game.

Alex nudged Sam and said, "Maybe we're in for more than just a drink tonight—perhaps some cosmic insight, too."

"I'm not sure exactly what all is covered in cosmology," Sam answered, "but it sounds like it might unveil some interesting mysteries."

Noticing their glances, Dr. Guillen approached with a warm, disarming smile. "Mind if I join you?" he asked, his tone inviting and relaxed. "I'm Michael Guillen."

"Pleased to meet you. I'm Sam, and this is my friend Alex."

"I couldn't help but overhear your discussion about cosmic mysteries a few moments ago," he said, his genuine interest immediately putting the two at ease. With a nod from Sam and a cautious smile from Alex, the three moved to a quieter corner where the ambient noise softened into a pleasant background hum.

After he sat, Dr. Guillen raised his glass in a spontaneous toast. "To cosmic curiosity." The clink of their glasses set the stage for an evening that promised both science and camaraderie.

"Tell us," Alex requested, "what are some of the cosmic mysteries cosmologists wrestle with?"

"I'd be glad to share a few with you," responded Dr. Guillen. "First, imagine the universe as a cosmic ocean that's endlessly vast. If you set sail from one star, you'd travel for trillions of miles and not even scratch the surface of this ultimate expanse. Picture galaxies, each a cosmic neighborhood with billions of stars, floating like islands in this immense sea. There are over two trillion of these galaxies! The universe is so colossal that light, the fastest thing we know, takes billions of years to journey from one end to another. In a nutshell, the universe is mind-bogglingly, unimaginably, and gloriously huge!"

Leaning back in his chair, Dr. Guillen continued: "Cosmology is like the grand detective story of the universe. Imagine trying to unravel the biggest mysteries of all time: Where did the universe come from, what is it made of, how did it evolve, and what will its future be? Cosmologists are the detectives of the cosmos. They look up into the vastness of space and time, seeking clues hidden in the stars, galaxies, and black holes to piece together the epic tale of our universe. In essence, cosmology is the study of the universe at its largest scales and earliest moments. It's like looking at the universe with a time machine, using the light traveling across space to peer back into the past."

Sam jumped in. "So when you use your time machine to peer into the past, where did the universe come from?"

Dr. Guillen leaned forward. "For centuries, we believed the universe was eternal—a static, unchanging backdrop. That idea was shattered in the early twentieth century." His eyes sparkled with enthusiasm as he recounted the pivotal breakthroughs that reshaped modern cosmology.

"In 1916, Einstein's general theory of relativity implied that the cosmos should be expanding. But at the time, to keep the old model intact, Einstein introduced what he called a 'cosmological constant'—a mathematical patch to force his equations into a static universe. Later, he called it his biggest mistake when the evidence for expansion became overwhelming."

Alex interjected with a wry smile, "So even Einstein had to compromise on his own theory?"

The group chuckled, and Dr. Guillen nodded. "Exactly," he said. "And then came Edwin Hubble.

"In 1926, while at the Wilson Observatory, Hubble observed that nearly every galaxy was moving away from Earth. He noticed the light from these galaxies was redshifted—shifted toward the red end of the spectrum—indicating an expanding universe. By 1929, Hubble's law was firmly established, showing that the farther a galaxy is, the faster it recedes. This discovery was a clear sign that the universe had a beginning."

Sam sipped his lager thoughtfully, picturing an expanding cosmos like a balloon being steadily inflated. "It's almost poetic," he mused, "to think that everything we see today was once squeezed into an unimaginably small point." The comment sparked memories of college debates with Alex—discussions where cosmic origins were pondered over late-night study sessions.

Alex's skepticism softened into genuine interest as he asked, "But if the universe is expanding, doesn't that mean it must have begun with some kind of explosive event? What evidence do we have that such an explosion actually happened?"

Dr. Guillen's smile deepened as he prepared to explain further. "In 1965, while working at Bell Laboratories, two scientists—Arno Penzias and Robert Wilson—encountered a persistent, low-level noise while testing a large microwave antenna. At first, they thought it was something as mundane as bird droppings interfering with their equipment, but soon they realized this noise was not a flaw at all. It was the cosmic microwave background radiation—the lingering afterglow of the Big Bang."

Alex's eyes widened. "So, the universe still carries the faint echo of its explosive birth?"

"Exactly," replied Dr. Guillen. "And to solidify this evidence, in 1990, NASA launched the Cosmic Background Explorer—COBE—to measure that radiation. The satellite's data confirmed that the background radiation was astonishingly uniform across the sky, a pattern that makes sense only if everything originated from one colossal explosion. It's like the universe was once a superheated, dense point that burst outward in every direction."

The bar's lively hum continued around them, but their table had become an island of focused conversation. Sam, probing further, asked, "If the universe had such an explosive start, where did the energy for that explosion come from?"

"A great question," responded Dr. Guillen. "Today many cosmologists support the quantum vacuum theory. Think of the universe as a magical, cosmic bubble that suddenly appeared out of nowhere. In this theory, we're looking at the weird and wonderful world of quantum physics, where tiny particles can spontaneously pop in and out of existence.

"One day, one of these fluctuations got a little too excited and poof!—a universe was born. In this grand scale of randomness, the Big Bang was like the ultimate cosmic lottery win. From this seeming 'nothing' came everything, painting a picture of creation that was as spontaneous and unpredictable as a spark in the dark."

He paused, letting his words sink in, while Alex considered the implications with a raised eyebrow. "So, the vacuum is not 'nothing' but a dynamic state, teeming with potential energy?"

"Exactly," replied Dr. Guillen. "Stephen Hawking, a leading atheist cosmologist, even argued that the laws of gravity might allow the universe to come into being from this quantum nothing- ness. Yet, if gravity itself can emerge from the vacuum, it raises the question: Where did gravity come from in the first place?"

"So," Sam asked, "you're saying something came from noth- ing? Like this table in front of us just appeared out of no place, because it turns out 'no place' was actually 'someplace'?"

"That's about it," responded Dr. Guillen. "So, in simple terms, the quantum vacuum theory is an intriguing idea about how our universe might have started from 'nothing,' but it remains speculative with no direct evidence to confirm that a quantum vacuum caused the Big Bang. Since we can't see or recreate the exact conditions from the beginning of the universe, proving this or any other theory is tricky."

"Does cosmology allow you to consider the possibility the universe was created by intelligent design?" asked Sam.

Sitting up and moving closer, Dr. Guillen replied, "I'm afraid science in general makes it a point to finding wholly rational explanations for everything. Explanations that involve God or other supernatural beings are viewed as 'superstitious' and generally unacceptable for scientific explanation.

"But it does seem more and more scientists are willing to consider a 'supernatural' creator, an intelligent designer. They think of the universe as a grand, ticking clock. It's intricate and precise, with planets spinning, stars burning, and galaxies swirling in perfect harmony. Just like a watch needs a watchmaker, the complexity and orderliness of the universe are leading more and more scientists to consider the evidence of a cosmic designer behind it all—a master craftsman who set everything ticking perfectly on purpose."

Dr. Guillen paused to take a drink from the ale he had ordered and then added, "Whether you see the Big Bang as the result of spontaneous quantum fluctuations or as evidence of a creative spark from a higher power, the journey of inquiry is an exciting road to pursue."

The background chatter of the bar and occasional bursts of laughter provided a gentle counterpoint to the deep questions posed at their table. Sam gazed out the large windows, where the inky night sky was dotted with countless stars. "Every time I look at the cosmos, I'm reminded that we're all just small parts of a much larger mystery. It's humbling, isn't it?"

Alex, his usual skepticism softened by the evening's discussion, nodded. "I still lean toward natural explanations, but I can't help but feel that the evidence—everything from the Big Bang's echo to the vast energy calculations—forces you to wonder if there's something more at work."

Dr. Guillen added, "That's the beauty of this quest. Science isn't just about gathering facts—it's about exploring the unknown, challenging our assumptions, and sometimes even reconciling what seems irreconcilable."

As the night deepened, the atmosphere at the bar mellowed. The clink of glasses, soft laughter, and gentle background music blended with the echoes of their profound conversation. Dr. Guillen eventually excused himself to join a small group heading to a stargazing event on the upper deck. Sam and Alex could hear the hum of ocean waves in the background.

Alex swirled the ice in his glass. "Well, that was a mind bender. I didn't expect to leave a cruise bar thinking about quantum fluctuations and Einstein's constant."

Sam grinned. "Yeah, Dr. Guillen has a way of making the universe feel both massive and personal at the same time."

"I have to admit," Alex reflected, "I've heard about the Big Bang before—but I didn't realize how unsettled the explanations still are. I always thought it was just settled science."

"And now?"

Alex shrugged. "I get that the quantum vacuum theory says something—some energy fluctuation in a preexisting quantum field—triggered the Big Bang. But it still begs the question: Where did that quantum field come from?"

Sam leaned in. "Exactly. A lot of people think that theory answers everything, but it just pushes the origin question one step back. It's like saying the match lit the fire without asking who struck the match."

Alex raised an eyebrow. "But doesn't intelligent design have its own problem? If you say a mind created everything, then who created the mind?"

Sam nodded slowly. "Fair question. But a key difference is this: Everything within the universe has a beginning and needs a cause. But whatever caused the universe itself must, by definition, exist outside of time, space, and matter—and be uncaused.

That's not a dodge; it's basic logic. The cause of everything can't be something that itself began. So, if the universe had a beginning—as the Big Bang suggests—then something eternal, immaterial, and powerful must've started it."

Alex sipped his drink, staring out at the sea. "That's a heavy thought. I mean, you're basically saying God is the most reasonable explanation for why anything exists at all."

Sam sat back in his chair. "That's the obvious conclusion."

"Still hard to get my head around. I lean more toward naturalistic explanations—not because they answer everything, but because at least they keep us grounded in what we can measure and test."

"But isn't that part of the problem? If you only accept what's testable, you might miss the deeper causes behind the curtain. The fact that something exists rather than nothing is a philosophical and metaphysical question as much as a scientific one."

Alex chuckled. "You're starting to sound like Dr. Morgan now. Between his talk on the laws of nature this morning and Dr. Guillen tonight . . . I'll admit, it's getting harder to dismiss the idea of intelligent design—God—out of hand."

Smiling, Sam said, "That's all about being open to the evidence, wherever it leads. Not to blind faith, but to the possibility that all of this—the stars, the laws, the life in your veins—is pointing to someone greater than ourselves."

Alex nodded slowly, "I'm not convinced . . . but I'm intrigued. I guess the universe is starting to feel a little more personal than it used to."

"And maybe that's the beginning of something bigger."

They fell into a quiet pause, letting the waves speak for a while. The stars above began to shimmer. Sam tried to interpret Alex's thoughtful look: Maybe somewhere between scientific rigor and wonder, a door in his friend's mind was starting to crack open.

QUESTION FOR REFLECTION: *If the universe had a beginning—as both science and philosophy suggest—what do you believe is the most reasonable explanation for its origin: an uncaused, personal creator outside of space and time, or a natural process with no guiding intelligence?*

CHAPTER 4
How Earth Got "Just Right"

THE NEXT MORNING, Sam and Alex met on the ship's promenade after breakfast. The scent of fresh coffee drifted by, and sunlight turned the ocean's surface into a glittering mosaic. Both men still had last night's discussion on their minds: Had the universe really started out of nothing, or was there something more intentional at work?

Sam scrolled through the day's lecture schedule on his phone. "Hey, here's a new talk by Dr. Morgan: 'The Fine-Tuned Universe.'"

Alex raised an eyebrow. "Fine-tuned? Like there's a cosmic engineer out there?"

"Or maybe just one big cosmic accident. Let's go see."

They headed inside, joining a procession of fellow passengers toward the lounge—by now a familiar venue. Floor-to-ceiling windows let in brilliant morning light, and a low hum of conversation filled the air.

Around thirty people had gathered. Sam and Alex slipped into seats near the front, where Dr. Morgan stood behind a lectern, leafing through his notes. He nodded in welcome upon recognizing two familiar faces. When the audience settled, he tapped the microphone.

"Good morning," he said. "In our previous session, we talked about the laws of nature. Today, we'll tackle a related question: Is our universe *fine-tuned* for life? And if so, who—or what—did the tuning?"

He paused, then flashed a disarming grin before continuing. "Imagine walking into a vacation rental and discovering everything set up just the way you like it. Wouldn't that be a pleasant surprise?"

Several people nodded and chuckled.

"After opening the door," Dr. Morgan went on, "you discover everything is set just for you—your favorite music is playing, the temperature is exactly seventy-two degrees, the fridge is stocked with your preferred snacks and drinks, and even the bathroom has your usual brand of shampoo. Would you chalk that up to pure chance, or suspect someone deliberately made it that way?"

Alex folded his arms, waiting to see how Dr. Morgan would connect this to the cosmos. Sam leaned forward, intrigued.

A slide flashed on the screen behind Dr. Morgan, showing an image of stars and galaxies. "In 1973, physicist Brandon Carter introduced the anthropic principle. He noticed that countless aspects of our universe appear meticulously set up for life, almost as if the cosmos 'expected' us. Later, Canadian astrophysicist Hugh Ross noted that by 2001, astronomers had identified over 150 finely tuned constants and conditions required for life."

He clicked to another slide listing a handful of these constants: gravitational force, electromagnetic force, the nuclear forces, and more. "Ross estimated the odds of all these characteristics lining up by random chance are so huge—about one in 10^{173}—that it might as well be infinite."

Sam glanced at Alex, who seemed clearly impressed by the sheer magnitude of those odds.

Dr. Morgan moved to a related topic. "An example of these constants would be the expansion rate of the universe right after the Big Bang. Eric Hedin, a professor of physics and astronomy, points out that if the universe expanded even slightly faster, matter would have spread out too thinly to form galaxies. If it expanded slower, it would've collapsed back into black holes. Either way, no life.

"Scientists estimate this expansion had to be tuned to within one part in 10^{60}. Think about that: One in 10^{60} is like picking the same single grain of sand out of all the beaches and deserts on Earth *three times in a row*. That number is mind-boggling, yet it's just one example among many."

A few murmurs rippled through the audience.

Dr. Morgan tapped his fingers on the lectern for emphasis. "Next, we have four fundamental forces in the universe: the strong nuclear force, weak nuclear force, electromagnetic force, and gravity. They determine how everything from the smallest atoms to the largest galaxies behaves. Each must fall within incredibly narrow ranges for life to exist.

"The first fundamental force, gravity, pulls objects toward each other. It's what holds us on the ground, makes apples fall from trees, and keeps the planets in orbit around the sun. The bigger the object, the stronger its gravitational pull. For example, Earth is much bigger than you, so it pulls you down towards it!

"Imagine a giant trampoline with a heavy ball in the center. The ball creates a dip in the trampoline, and if you roll a smaller ball nearby, it will roll toward the heavy ball because of the dip. This is like how gravity works in space!

"If the force of gravity were any stronger, stars would burn hot and die fast. If weaker, they'd never ignite. Stephen Hawking called it remarkable how precisely balanced these forces are to allow life."

Dr. Morgan paused to allow listeners a moment to process the information before moving on. "The second force is the electromagnetic force which is responsible for electricity and magnetism. It holds atoms together and is what makes things stick to each other, like how a magnet sticks to your fridge. This force is also why we can feel the heat from the sun and why we can see colors.

"Picture two magnets. When you try to push the same poles, say, two north poles, together, they repel each other. And when you bring opposite poles—north and south—close, they attract. This is how electromagnetic force works!

"If the electromagnetic force didn't have the right strength, electrons wouldn't orbit nuclei. Too high or too low, you'd never get atoms bonding into molecules. No molecules, no life.

"The strong nuclear force is the third force. This holds the particles in the nucleus of an atom together. It's incredibly powerful but only works across very short distances, like inside an atom. Without this force, atoms would fall apart, and matter as we know it wouldn't exist.

"Think of a group of tiny balls, representing protons and neutrons, packed tightly in a small box, or the nucleus of the atom. The strong nuclear force is like a super-strong glue that keeps those balls from flying apart, even though they're pushing against each other! If the strong nuclear force were even slightly weaker, only hydrogen could form. If stronger, elements lighter than iron would be almost nonexistent.

"The fourth force is the weak nuclear force, which is responsible for some types of radioactive decay and is crucial in nuclear reactions, like those that power the sun. It's called 'weak' because it's much weaker than the strong nuclear force, but it plays an important role in how particles interact and change.

"Imagine a game of Jenga where one block, representing a particle, slowly tips and falls off the tower, or the atom. The weak nuclear force is like a gentle nudge that causes that block to fall. It changes the structure of the tower over time, similar to how the weak force changes particles in an atom.

"Too strong or too weak, and you'd get the wrong amount of helium—or none at all—meaning no stars, no planets."

Sam raised his hand. "So, Dr. Morgan," he asked, "these are universal 'settings,' basically?"

"Exactly," Dr. Morgan replied. "Like knobs on a control panel—each one must be dialed in *just so.*"

With another click, Earth itself appeared on the screen: a swirl of blue oceans and green landmasses. "We also have *planetary* fine-tuning. Jupiter, thanks to its massive gravity, sucks in or deflects dangerous debris that might otherwise crash into Earth. Our moon stabilizes Earth's rotation, creating predictable tides that help purify the oceans.

"And Earth orbits in the so-called 'Goldilocks zone,' not too hot, not too cold. Our sun emits just the right spectrum for photosynthesis. More than 70 percent of Earth's surface is water, crucial for life. The atmosphere strikes a perfect balance of gases to trap heat, filter radiation, and provide oxygen. Even our 23.5-degree axial tilt gives us seasons, allowing diverse climates for farming."

Dr. Morgan paused, scanning the listeners. "So, how did the universe—and Earth in particular—acquire these unique constants needed for life? Paul Davies, a prominent physicist who spent decades searching for naturalist answers, calls the physical evidence for design 'overwhelming.' It's like the entire universe is a Vrbo prepped for life."

Alex raised his hand. "What about the multiverse idea? Maybe there are infinite universes, and ours just happens to have all the right constants."

Dr. Morgan nodded. "Yes, that's a leading naturalist alternative. Inflationary cosmology suggests our universe might be one bubble among countless others. If you have an infinite number of universes, the reasoning goes, eventually one of them will have precisely the conditions necessary for life."

Sam chimed in: "But is there evidence for these other universes?"

"None so far," Dr. Morgan answered. "Critics point out that the multiverse concept isn't testable or falsifiable—two key criteria for scientific inquiry. Antony Flew, an atheist turned theist, argued that just because multiple universes are *logically* possible doesn't mean they *actually* exist."

Dr. Morgan wrapped up his slides. "So, do we live in a universe that's fine-tuned by a divine creator, or are we just cosmic lottery winners in an infinite sea of universes? Science won't hand us a neat answer on a silver platter. But these facts certainly raise big questions about the nature of reality and our place in it."

He stepped away from the lectern while applause rose from the audience. People drifted into small groups, buzzing with debate. Sam and Alex lingered near the broad windows that revealed the shimmering ocean.

Alex, shaking his head slightly, raised his eyebrows. "Well . . . I've got to admit, Dr. Morgan made a strong case. Those numbers were staggering."

"You mean the odds of the universe being this finely tuned for life?"

"Yeah," said Alex. "I mean, gravity, the strong nuclear force, dark energy—all of it balanced so precisely. It's . . . pretty amazing."

Sam grinned. "'Amazing' is a good word. Like Dr. Morgan said, 'the universe was actually expecting us.'"

"Or . . . we just happen to live in one lucky universe out of trillions," Alex replied.

"Ah yes," Sam chuckled, "the multiverse card."

"I'm not saying it *has* to be true. But if there's an infinite number of universes out there, it makes sense that eventually one would randomly get all the right settings for life—like ours."

"Look, I get the logic. If chance gets enough rolls of the dice, something extraordinary eventually happens. But let me ask you—how would we ever *know* those other universes exist?"

Thinking aloud, Alex responded, "We might not. At least not directly. But some physicists think certain patterns or mathematical predictions could point to a multiverse, even if we can't see it."

"That could be," Sam countered, "but if a theory can't be tested or observed, doesn't it sound a lot more like philosophy, speculation—or even faith—than science?"

"Maybe, but isn't belief in a designer the same thing? Faith filling in the gaps?"

"I think there's a difference. We actually have evidence of design—right here in this universe. The precision of conditions in the universe needed for life, the fine-tuned constants. In everyday life, if we see a code or a machine calibrated to perform just right, we naturally assume design, not accident."

Alex half grinned. "Unless there's a universe-making machine churning out failures by the trillion until one finally hits the jackpot."

Sam smiled, appreciative of the banter. "Okay, fair. But even that machine would need rules, structure—some kind of framework to operate. And that raises a deeper question: Who or what designed *that*?"

"So, you're saying whether it's one universe or a multiverse, design is still built in?"

"That's where I land. At some point, you still have to ask—why is there something instead of nothing? And why is it so ordered, so tuned, and so strangely welcoming to conscious life capable of asking the question?"

Alex looked out over the water. "You know, Dr. Morgan is making me think harder than I expected."

Sam smiled and placed his hand on Alex's shoulder. "That's more than enough for today."

QUESTION FOR REFLECTION: *If the universe truly appears "fine-tuned," does it suggest a cosmic designer, or could the multiverse—or some other natural explanation—account for these astronomically precise conditions?*

CHAPTER 5

Who Authored the DNA Code?

S UNLIGHT POURED INTO the ship's dining hall, gleaming off rows of polished silverware. Sam and Alex were finishing breakfast at a small table by the window, their plates cleared away. The previous day's conversation about the universe's fine-tuning still lingered in the back of their minds.

Alex tapped the edge of his coffee mug. "So we've talked about cosmic laws and the Big Bang. What's next—do we dissect a cell?"

Sam scrolled through his phone's lecture schedule. "Funny you say that. There's a session this morning: 'DNA: The Instruction Book of Life.'"

Alex raised an eyebrow. "Another lecture from Dr. Morgan?"

"Actually, no. It's someone else—Dr. Marie Caldwell, a molecular biologist, I think."

Despite Alex's skepticism, it was evident he was becoming hooked by these daily talks. Together, they made their way to the same mid-level lounge where rows of chairs faced a small stage.

This time, a modest group of about twenty people had gathered, giving the room a cozy feel.

Dr. Caldwell, a lean woman in her fifties with salt-and-pepper hair tied in a loose bun, stepped forward. She welcomed everyone warmly, then—without preamble—began with an anecdote that made Alex's eyes widen.

"Have any of you heard of Antony Flew?" she asked, surveying the crowd. A few hands went up. "He was, for decades, one of the most influential atheists in the world—a real intellectual giant who argued against God's existence. Then, in a debate at New York University, he shocked everyone by announcing he'd changed his mind. He now believed in a God."

Sam glanced at Alex, who furrowed his brow.

Dr. Caldwell pressed on. "Flew later explained that new origin-of-life findings—especially regarding DNA—had convinced him. In his words: 'By the almost unbelievable complexity of the arrangements which are needed to produce life, intelligence must have been involved.' If that quote piques your curiosity, you're in the right place."

The lights dimmed slightly as Dr. Caldwell clicked to her first slide: an image of the famous DNA double helix. "For many, DNA is just that 'fingerprint' law enforcement uses to match suspects to crimes. But it's so much more. DNA is a chemical code telling each cell how to function, reproduce, and thrive."

She showed a simplified cell diagram. "Back when I was a student," she admitted with a laugh, "we drew cells like sunny-side-up eggs—just a nucleus in the middle, cytoplasm around it. Darwin himself envisioned something similar, describing the cell in pretty simplistic terms."

A second slide displayed a high-powered electron microscope's image of a cell's interior. Intricate molecular machines crowded every corner—like a bustling factory assembly line. "Today," Dr.

Caldwell explained, "we know each cell is a 3D factory full of specialized machines. And the master control office? That's DNA, transmitting instructions through a carefully coded language."

Dr. Caldwell tapped the screen to reveal a graphic comparing Morse code to DNA's four-letter alphabet. "In the 1800s, Samuel Morse created a code of dots and dashes because he couldn't send full words over a telegraph. DNA does something similar but with four chemical 'letters': A, G, C, and T. Strung together in the right sequence, they form instructions that tell a cell how to build amino acids, then proteins, then entire body structures."

She paused to let that sink in. "The complexity is staggering. A molecular machine unwinds the DNA, another copies it into messenger RNA, which then goes to the ribosome—a 'factory line'—where amino acids form chains. If you get one base wrong in a chain of twelve hundred or more, you can end up with a useless protein."

Glancing at her notes, she added, "Bill Gates once remarked, 'DNA is like a software program, only much more complex than anything we've ever devised.' Makes you think: A code usually requires a coder."

The next slide showed photos of Stanley Miller and Harold Urey, the scientists who, in 1953, famously tried to replicate early Earth conditions. "Maybe you remember the 'prebiotic soup' concept from your school days," Dr. Caldwell said. "Miller and Urey removed oxygen from a flask, filled it with methane, ammonia, and hydrogen, then zapped it with electricity. They got amino acids—'the building blocks of proteins.' Some took that as proof you could get life from non-life."

Alex leaned over and whispered to Sam, "Yeah, I remember that from biology class. Everyone acted like it settled the question."

Dr. Caldwell continued, "But there are three major issues. First, more recent geology suggests Earth's early atmosphere likely had oxygen—so the experiment's assumptions might be off. If that were the case, the results would not have been amino acids but a big gooey mess.

"Second, making amino acids is not the same as making a living, self-replicating cell. That would require instructions—DNA or something like it. Third, these experiments never produced a functional code. It's like discovering a pile of building materials but no blueprint to make a real house."

She clicked to a text slide quoting Harvard chemist George Whitesides: "We believe life emerged spontaneously. How? I have no idea." With a slight shrug, Dr. Caldwell said, "That's the crux: No natural process has demonstrated how raw chemistry turns into information—the coded instructions that make cells alive."

"Some folks say," she went on, "that given enough time, chance could do it. They use the analogy of a million monkeys typing randomly until they produce Shakespeare. But one experiment locked a computer keyboard in a cage with six monkeys for a month; they produced fifty pages—*not a single real word*, not even A or I. If you extend that to an entire Shakespearean sonnet, the odds become one in 10^{690}. Remember," she added with a grin, "the total number of particles in the universe—protons, neutrons, electrons—is around 10^{80}. So that's some real long odds."

Dr. Caldwell let that hang for a moment before moving on. "And DNA is even more complex than a Shakespearean sonnet. So, you see why a lifelong atheist like Antony Flew said the arrangement of these chemical letters can't be blind luck."

A new voice spoke up from the audience, belonging to a younger man with an ID badge identifying him as "Dr. Tim Patel, Biochemistry." "Evolutionary theory suggests species change bit by bit. Couldn't small mutations add new instructions over time?"

Dr. Caldwell acknowledged the question. "That's the standard idea, yes. But as biophysicist Lee Spitner and others have pointed out, beneficial mutations typically *rearrange* or *lose* existing data. Gaining brand-new coding—like going from reptile scales to bird feathers—requires a blueprint not found in the original DNA. And if random typos are more likely to break text than write a new chapter, how do we explain entire new structures?"

She gave a polite shrug. "I'm not saying microevolution or adaptation doesn't happen. But turning one major form of life into a completely new one means adding instructions that aren't there. That's a separate challenge from just 'tweaking' what's already present."

Looping back to the opening story, Dr. Caldwell said, "So, why did Antony Flew shift from atheism to theism? He summed it up simply: 'I had to go where the evidence leads.' In his case, DNA's complexity was the tipping point. Of course, many scientists, like George Wald, choose to believe that life emerged spontaneously, no matter how unlikely. Each of us has to weigh the data and decide."

She switched off the projector, stepping away from the lectern. "I hope I've at least made you curious enough to see how deep this rabbit hole goes."

Applause rippled through the small lounge. Sam and Alex stood, exchanging thoughtful looks. As they filed toward the exit, Dr. Patel caught up with them.

"Fascinating talk," he said, tucking a notepad under his arm. "I'll admit I'm more open to the idea of a designer than I used to be. DNA's code is . . . hard to explain with purely random chemistry."

Sam nodded. "It is. If a code requires an author, who wrote this one?"

Alex, though still reserved, seemed less dismissive than usual. "I'm not ready to jump to God as the answer, but the complexity's undeniable."

They emerged into the hallway, where sunlight streamed through circular portholes. Sam and Alex stood for a moment, letting the day's lecture settle in. Somewhere lower down, the ship's engine hummed softly, reminding them they were on a steady voyage—across the sea as well as through an equally vast sea of ideas.

Alex was clearly impressed. "I'll admit, that was fascinating. I didn't realize how incredibly complex a single cell really is."

"I didn't either. I mean, Darwin thought the cell was just a blob of protoplasm—a simple building block. But given what we know now, it's more like a miniature city running with software."

"That analogy about the DNA being like a four-letter alphabet writing instruction manuals blew my mind a little. Billions of characters, all ordered, all working together . . ."

Sam nodded. "Exactly. The fact that every cell in your body carries a set of encoded instructions more complex than any computer program—and it all fits into something microscopic."

Alex paused, then said half-joking, "But complexity doesn't necessarily mean design. Natural selection works on complex systems. We just understand more of the machinery now."

Sam smiled. "Sure, but that's the thing—natural selection *acts on* information. It doesn't *create* it. DNA isn't just complex—it carries *meaning*. Specific instructions. That's not something random chemistry can account for. We have to ask, 'How did mindless matter come to write a billion-letter instruction manual to build a human body? And why does it look so much like language? Why is it that when we map DNA, it doesn't just function—it communicates?'"

Alex was quiet for a moment. "It's compelling, I'll give you that. It feels like there's something more at play—but that doesn't prove God."

"True," Sam replied, "DNA doesn't spell out 'Made by God'— but it does raise the question: Is there an author behind the code of life?"

Alex looked out the porthole window at the endless blue of sky and ocean. "You know . . . for a long time, I told myself that science would eventually explain everything. Life, consciousness, meaning. I thought we just needed more time."

Sam remembered also feeling this way, adding, "That's what I used to think too. Until I realized science can describe how things work, but it doesn't always explain *why* they exist in the first place."

"Yeah . . . and today, sitting in that lecture, hearing how DNA operates like language—like an actual written code—I felt something I haven't felt in a long time."

"What was that?"

Alex was thoughtful. "Wonder. And maybe . . . a little doubt. Not in the science—but in the story I've always told myself. That life is just chemistry and chance."

"Sometimes doubt is just the start of a deeper kind of search."

Alex half-laughed. "From what I've heard the first two days, I was willing to consider the possibility of intelligent design. But now, after the presentation by Dr. Caldwell on DNA, although I'm not ready to say I believe in God, for the first time in a long time, I'm not so sure he *doesn't* exist."

"That's an honest place to be. God's not afraid of your questions. He's not asking you to leap blindly. He's inviting you to look, to listen—and to follow the evidence wherever it leads."

The waves rolled gently beneath them, but Sam could tell something deeper was moving inside Alex. Not an argument won. Not a debate resolved. But the quiet, unmistakable sound of a door beginning to open.

They stood in silence for a few moments, the breeze picking up around them. Perhaps somewhere deep inside Alex, questions were surfacing—no longer just about data, but about meaning. And Sam, quietly, was there to walk with him as those questions found their shape.

> QUESTION FOR REFLECTION: *If DNA truly behaves like a coded language, does this imply an intelligent author, or can random, natural processes alone account for the sophisticated instructions that underlie all life?*

CHAPTER 6

Where Consciousness Resides

LATE MORNING SUNLIGHT shimmered on the water as Sam and Alex strolled along the promenade deck. The breeze carried an invigorating hint of salt, and the distant horizon seemed endlessly far away. Sam's phone buzzed with a message from an old college friend—a reminder about their upcoming college reunion.

Sam sighed, pausing by the railing. "Remember last time we went to our college reunion? They read the names of classmates who passed away. It felt . . . heavy."

Alex leaned forward, peering at the ocean's expanse. "Yeah. Made me realize we're not immortal. Hard to believe people our age are already gone."

They both fell quiet, absorbing the reality that someday they, too, would be on such a list. Just then, a voice interrupted them. "Excuse me. Either of you have a spare pen? I've been doing some writing and my pen gave out."

Turning, they found themselves face to face with a woman in her forties, dressed casually in jeans and a windbreaker embroidered with a small university emblem. She had dark hair pulled into a ponytail and carried a small journal.

"Sure," Sam said, fishing a ballpoint from his pocket. "Here you go."

"Thanks." She flashed a quick grin. "I'm Marla Lane, by the way. I'm here on a sort of working holiday—trying to find a little peace and quiet to finish some research."

Alex raised an eyebrow. "Research? On a cruise?"

Marla shrugged good-naturedly. "Sometimes a change of scenery helps. I'm a psychologist—specializing in near-death experiences. My colleagues joke that I never take a real vacation."

Sam and Alex exchanged a quick glance. The question of what happens after death had been lingering in their minds—and now, by coincidence or something more, they were talking to someone who studied it for a living. It felt too timely to ignore.

"I'm Sam, and this is my friend Alex. Funny enough, we've been talking about that very topic—what happens after we die. We don't want to impose, but after you're finished with your work, would you care to join us for a latte on the aft deck? We'd love to hear about your research."

Marla smiled. "I'd be delighted. How about I join you in a couple of hours?"

"Perfect," Sam replied. "We'll see you there."

Two hours later, Marla stepped through the door of the coffee bar. Sam and Alex were seated at a table tucked away from the wind. Sam spotted her and waved her over. She joined them with a warm smile, and the three settled in, sipping from their steaming cups as the ship quietly cut through the open sea.

Sam broke the silence. "We've been talking about how short life is. A friend reminded me about our college reunion—some people we know are already gone." He paused, measuring his words. "I guess we're wondering, what happens next?"

Marla nodded compassionately. "It's the ultimate question. And, well, there's no single, unanimously accepted answer. But I can share some things I've learned."

She set down her cup. "Ever heard of Dr. Bruce Greyson at the University of Virginia? He started out as a psychiatric resident who had this bizarre experience with a patient. The story goes, he dripped mustard on his tie one night while rushing to the ER."

Sam and Alex listened intently as Marla described Holly, a college freshman who had overdosed and been found unconscious. "She couldn't have seen him that night—she was sedated, out cold. Yet, the next day, she mentioned the yellow smear on his tie and even described him chatting in the next room with her roommate. He had no clue how she knew."

Alex leaned forward, elbows on the table. "So that's what kicked off Greyson's interest in near-death experiences?"

"Exactly," Marla confirmed. "He realized something about human consciousness might extend beyond the brain's normal functioning. Holly should've been oblivious, yet she recalled events from when she was clinically unresponsive."

Sam took a slow sip and then asked, "So, how do you explain something like that?"

Marla shrugged. "Broadly speaking, there are two main ideas. One, the naturalist view: Our brain creates consciousness, so once the brain stops, that's the end. Stephen Hawking famously compared the brain to a computer—no afterlife for a broken machine. The second idea is that the mind—call it a soul, if you want—exists independently, even if it uses the brain as a vehicle."

She glanced out the window. "I'm not a fan of straw-man arguments. There are smart folks on both sides. Some say the mind is purely physical, others argue there's a spiritual dimension.

But after seeing enough cases, I'm leaning toward mind and brain being distinct."

"Because of near-death experiences?" Alex asked.

Marla nodded. "That, and other data. For instance, G.K. Chesterton made a point once: If naturalism is totally true, our thoughts are just atoms firing randomly, so how do we trust them to find truth?

"And then there's the work of neurosurgeon Wilder Penfield. He was one of the leading brain researchers of the twentieth century. During brain surgery on conscious patients—because the brain itself doesn't feel pain—he applied electrical stimulation to various parts of the brain. When he stimulated motor areas, their arms or legs would move involuntarily."

Alex nodded. "Right. That shows the brain controls the body."

"True—but here's the key part," Dr. Lane replied. "Every time Penfield made their limbs move, the patients always said, 'I didn't do that—you did that.' They clearly recognized the movement was not initiated by their own will. He could make their bodies act, but he couldn't force a choice, a decision, or a belief. He couldn't stimulate a sense of 'I will do this now.' The conscious self—their will—remained distinct."

Alex nodded more slowly, processing. "So you're saying the brain is like hardware, but the will—the 'self'—is something else entirely?"

"Exactly," Dr. Lane said. "Penfield himself concluded that the mind and the will can't be fully explained by brain activity alone. There seems to be a conscious agent—what many would call the soul—standing outside the physical machinery, making genuine choices. It's not just neurons firing; it's something more."

Marla warmed her hands on her latte cup. "Let me share another story—this one's from a Dr. Mary Neal, an orthopedic surgeon. She was kayaking in Chile and nearly drowned when her boat got pinned underwater at a waterfall. She describes floating out of her body, meeting angelic beings, seeing radiant color, feeling a rush of incredible love. Then, she was told it wasn't her time. She'd been submerged for about fifteen minutes before anyone rescued her. By all logic, she should've been gone. But she came back, and her life changed drastically."

Alex let out a low whistle. "Hard to dismiss that without calling her a liar or delusional."

Marla shrugged. "She's a well-credentialed doctor, not some thrill seeker making up fairy tales. People like her talk about these experiences as more real than anything they've felt in normal life."

"But we can't just *assume* those stories mean we have souls that float around," Alex protested. "Couldn't it be chemical—oxygen deprivation in a near-death state?"

Marla gave him a respectful nod. "Yes, that's the standard explanation. But plenty of these individuals recount details they *shouldn't* have if it were just brain chemistry. Like Dr. Greyson's patient, Holly, seeing things while unconscious."

She took a thoughtful pause. "And Dr. Greyson's compiled thousands of such accounts worldwide—cutting across cultures, ages, religious backgrounds. They report consistent themes: meeting deceased loved ones, feeling separated from time, encountering intense love or light. Many come back changed—more compassionate, less afraid of dying."

"So, what are the implications?" Sam asked.

Marla answered slowly, "Science hasn't pinned down how a physical organ—the brain—could generate subjective awareness, let alone consciousness beyond brain activity. Philosopher Alva Noe admits we haven't a clue. Physicist Nick Herbert calls consciousness the biggest mystery. And it's not just random fringe folks saying that; these are heavy-hitting academics."

She finished her latte and then said, "As for me, I'd say the evidence points to our minds being more than neural wiring. If that's true, maybe we don't vanish when our brains flatline."

A gentle hush followed. Alex was quiet, as if letting the idea settle in before speaking again. "My college reunion," he finally said, "the memorial for classmates—it makes me wonder if, in some form, they're still . . . out there."

"Or with God," Sam said. "If near-death experiences are real, it definitely shoots down the idea that we're just meat machines."

Marla smiled kindly. "I believe it does. Some people interpret it through the lens of biblical teaching—Genesis 2, humans made in God's image. Others see it as purely spiritual without tying it to a specific religion. Either way, it challenges the notion that we're nothing but neurons."

She rose, gathering her journal. "I should let you guys go about your day. But thanks for hearing me out. It's not easy research—there's skepticism from every angle. But I'd rather follow the data than ignore it."

Sam and Alex walked Marla to the café entrance. They thanked her for the conversation, parted ways, and stepped back into the open air of the promenade.

Alex reflected some more and then said, "The only article I've read about near-death experiences suggests it's just the brain's last electrical flares before shutting down. Chemicals firing, trying to protect the mind as it dies."

"But what do you do with the near-death accounts where people report things they couldn't have known—like conversations happening in another room, or describing details from surgeries while they were clinically brain dead?"

Alex shrugged. "I think the brain's more powerful than we understand. Maybe some kind of unconscious perception is still going on. But when the brain stops, *we* stop. Consciousness is a product of the machine."

Sam pushed back. "Unless consciousness isn't *just* a product of the machine. What if the brain is like hardware—and the soul is the user? When the hardware fails, the user isn't gone . . . just disconnected."

"You really believe there's a soul—something separate from the body?" Alex asked, squinting slightly.

Sam responded with a quiet conviction. "I do. And NDEs are just one thread pointing that way. We're more than neurons and synapses. There's something in us that longs for eternity—and maybe that's because we were made for it."

Alex gazed out at the dark sea, his voice low. "Or maybe that longing is just part of the program. A survival instinct. A way to soften the idea of nothingness."

"Or maybe it's there because we're not meant to be just dust and wiring. Think about it—why would evolution program us to long for something that doesn't exist? Justice. Meaning. Eternity. If all we are is biology, those things don't really matter. But if we're souls—created for more—they matter *because* they're real."

"And that's where God comes in?"

"Yeah. That's the core of it for me. If near-death experiences are even a glimpse of something beyond—something conscious, consistent, even *relational*—then that points not just to survival after death, but to God who made us for life that doesn't end."

Alex's reply was thoughtful. "I can't ignore how it connects with everything else we've been talking about."

Sam smiled. "And maybe that's the beginning of seeing the whole story. Not just what we're made of—but *who* we're made by . . . and *why*."

They remained there a moment longer, while the sea wind stirred around thoughts about mortality, the possibility of a mind that transcends the body, and what that might mean for each passing day a person draws breath.

QUESTION FOR REFLECTION: *If consciousness can persist even when the brain is severely compromised or clinically "dead," does that support the idea we have a soul distinct from our physical bodies—and possibly hint at a God who endowed us with that soul?*

CHAPTER 7

Why Pain and Suffering?

THE NEXT DAY a calm stillness settled over the SS *Aurora's* lounge as Sam and Alex sat by the window in the late afternoon sun. They sipped their drinks slowly, the lime catching the light as the hum of the ship drifted beneath them.

Alex stared out at the sea. "You know, Sam . . . this whole week has been something I didn't expect. I came here curious, maybe even a little cynical. But now?" He paused. "It's getting harder to say all this is just random chance. I think—I'm starting to believe there really is a God behind it all."

He turned to face Sam and added, "But there's still one thing that keeps me from fully stepping across the line. If God really is there—and if he's good and all-powerful—then why does he allow so much pain? Kids with cancer. Natural disasters. Abuse. Genocide. Either he can stop it and doesn't . . . or he can't. Either way, it's hard to call him good."

"That's one of the hardest questions anyone can ask, Alex. And it's one I've wrestled with myself—not just intellectually, but personally. And yeah, it's the classic dilemma: If God is all-powerful, he could stop suffering. If he's all-good, he'd want to. Given that, maybe people should say that he's not truly powerful or good—or simply that he doesn't exist at all. It's definitely a complex puzzle."

"It certainly is," came a quiet voice from the table next to them.

They turned to see a woman in her fifties with short, graying hair and weary eyes. She wore a simple cardigan and held a mug of tea in her hands.

"I hope I'm not intruding," she said, "but I've wrestled with that question for years—both personally and in my work. I'm Sara Wolfe, a professor of philosophy."

"I'm Sam, and this is my friend Alex. We'd love to hear your perspective on solving the puzzle. Would you like to join us?"

"I'd love to," Sara said, pulling out the empty chair next to them and setting her drink on the table. "I'm here with some friends . . . but I also needed some personal space. My life took a rough turn three years ago when I lost my husband. He was healthy, he loved God—didn't do anything to deserve suffering. And yet . . ." She swallowed. "He got an aggressive neurological disease, and in a few short months, he was gone."

Alex exhaled softly. "I'm really sorry."

Sara's gaze moved from Alex to Sam. "Thank you. Those months left me wrestling with your exact question: How can an all-powerful, good God allow awful things to happen to people who didn't do anything wrong? There were nights I screamed that at the sky, convinced God must be either uncaring or incapable of helping."

Sara took a quiet sip of her tea, gathering her thoughts. "My years in the field of philosophy," she finally said, "could not really answer the question at a personal level. But over time, I pieced together some perspectives—biblical and otherwise—that helped me not only stay afloat but eventually find hope."

Alex and Sam exchanged a glance. Then Sam said, "Please, go on."

Sara clasped her hands. "First off, I realized my outrage—'How could God let this happen?'—implied a sense that something wasn't *right*. But if the universe were random, purely material, why do we assume there's a 'right' way at all? Why do we cry out, 'It's not fair!' if there's no moral line in the first place?"

Alex rubbed his chin. "You mean if there's no objective good, we wouldn't feel *wronged* by bad things?"

"Exactly," Sara said. "C. S. Lewis, the great Christian apologist, phrased it like this: We call a line crooked because we know what straight is. Our moral outrage at innocent suffering hints that deep down, we believe there *should* be justice—something bigger than chance. That doesn't solve the problem, but it made me see that evil doesn't necessarily disprove God. It can, oddly enough, point to a standard we think God ought to uphold."

Alex adjusted in his seat. "Okay, so moral outrage might show there's a moral law. But that still doesn't explain how a loving, powerful God can watch people suffer for no fault of their own—like your husband."

Sara's eyes flickered with sadness. "I know. Often, we talk about free will—how God allows people to choose good or evil. That explains human-caused suffering like wars or abuse. God could forcibly stop it, but then we'd lose real choice. And love wouldn't be genuine if we were puppets. But," she admitted, "that doesn't fully address things like my husband's disease or natural disasters. Those aren't caused by a person's evil choice."

She continued, "The Bible claims creation itself is disrupted—'fallen' since humanity's rebellion against God. That leads to diseases, disasters, suffering that's not anyone's direct fault. If we ask, 'Why doesn't God fix it instantly?' the Christian view is that he's *in the process* of doing so, but we're not at the final stage yet."

Alex let out a breath. "That's where the question arises: If he's truly all-powerful, why wait? Doesn't that mean either he can't fix it or he won't?"

Sara nodded. "I asked the same thing. Some say if God doesn't step in immediately, he must be uncaring or weak. But the biblical narrative suggests a bigger plan—one where God patiently addresses both moral evil and creation's brokenness. If he just wiped out all suffering right now, he'd also wipe out freedom and the potential for genuine relationships. There's a tension here, and it's not neatly resolved. Yet, believers see glimpses of God's power in miracles, in Jesus's healings, in modern testimonies—but it's not universal at this time. Scripture points to a future restoration."

She sighed, her voice trembling with emotion. "Please understand, I'd never say, 'God caused my husband's sickness to teach me a lesson.' But in that dark valley, I grew in ways I never would have otherwise. I learned empathy for others who suffer, found a deeper reliance on God, and recognized how fragile life is. Many who face hardship say they discover a compassion, an unselfishness that a comfortable life rarely produces."

"But does that mean God does use suffering just to shape you?" Alex asked.

A sorrowful smile touched her lips. "No. I believe he weeps with us, that suffering wasn't his original design. Yet he can *redeem* our pain. For me, that redemption was turning my grief into a calling—volunteering at a hospice, comforting those who feel abandoned."

She inhaled slowly. "Evil isn't good, but God can bring good out of it, if we let him."

Alex swallowed. "It's one thing to say God's not done with the world. But is he really near, or is that just wishful thinking?"

Sara looked him in the eye. "I thought so too—until I felt an inexplicable peace in the ICU, praying over my husband when he was unconscious. It didn't fix his disease, but I sensed I wasn't alone. The Gospels paint Jesus as someone who wept at Lazarus's tomb, faced unimaginable pain on the cross. That's not a distant clockmaker God—it's one who *enters* suffering."

Sam nodded. "A God who's all-powerful but also shares our pain. That's . . . comforting, in a strange way."

"And the final piece that helped me," Sara added, "was seeing existence as a two-act play. Act 1 is our broken world, with some glimpses of God's intervention but not complete justice. Act 2, the Bible says, is a future reality where evil is judged, the world's restored, and suffering ends."

Alex frowned. "So innocent people might still die unfairly now, and we just have to wait for Act 2?"

Sara nodded sadly. "It sounds harsh, but it also means we aren't stuck with the conclusion that God doesn't care or isn't strong enough. If there's another act, then cosmic justice is postponed, not denied. My husband's suffering was real; the heartbreak is real, but I cling to the hope that God will set things right in the end—that he's not 'hands off.' He's waiting for reasons we can't fully see, giving humans time to turn to him, weaving a bigger story."

Sara paused and then addressed the elephant in the room: "So does that mean God's either not loving or not all-powerful? Honestly, I see it differently: If he weren't loving, he'd never bother to be with us in our pain or promise future restoration. If he weren't powerful, he couldn't have created the universe or done any miracles at all. The story of the Bible claims he's both but chooses not to forcibly erase evil at this stage, lest he erase our freedom and capacity for love along with it."

She drew a shaky breath. "It's a mystery, but for me, it's more plausible than thinking there's no God or that he's too weak or cruel. Especially after experiencing deep comfort and a sense of God walking through the valley with me."

They all fell silent, the hum of the lounge filling the space. Finally, Sam spoke: "Sara that's . . . powerful. Hearing how you faced the loss of someone who did nothing to deserve it—I'm sorry you had to endure that."

Alex nodded, and with a low voice, said, "It's the hardest question: Why innocent people? If your husband was a good man—" He trailed off, struggling for the right words.

Sara offered them a sad, gentle smile. "I still ache every day. But you know, I no longer see suffering as a reason to dismiss God. Instead, I see it as a reason to seek him more—believing he's good *and* powerful, that he has a plan bigger than Act 1, and that he's not indifferent to our pain."

A few more moments passed before Sara glanced at her watch. "I'm sorry—I'm meeting friends soon. I hope this conversation helps even a little."

Sam stood, shaking her hand. "It does. Thank you for being so open."

Alex added, "I appreciate your candor—and your willingness to address the all-loving, all-powerful question. That's been one of my sticking points."

Sara nodded. "You might not get a perfect, logical wrap-up, but I hope you see that Christian theology at least provides a framework: free will, a fallen world, a God who enters our pain, and a future resolution. No quick fix, but genuine hope."

They watched Sara depart, a hush remaining in her wake. Sam and Alex returned to their seats, the weight of her testimony settling in.

Sam murmured, "Seeing Sara's pain made it real. Yet she still trusts God. If she can find hope after that experience, that makes a strong statement."

Alex swirled his drink. "After seeing her heart and listening to her words, I can see how God might be both good and powerful—working in ways we don't fully grasp yet."

The conversation drifted, yet the import of Sara's words lingered: Sometimes, the best answer to suffering isn't a tidy formula but a story of a God who cares enough to suffer with us, who promises that in Act 2, every unjust moment will somehow find resolution.

> QUESTION FOR REFLECTION: *If God is truly all-powerful and all-loving, how do we make sense of innocent suffering? Does Sara's journey—recognizing free will, a fallen creation, God's empathy, and a future Act 2— offer a plausible reconciliation?*

CHAPTER 8

Is the Bible Reliable?

THE NEXT DAY Sam was in his cabin, feeling the gentle rock-
ing of the SS *Aurora* beneath his feet and noticing beams of
sunlight slipping through the curtain in soft, golden streaks.
He glanced at his watch—just enough time to get ready to meet
Alex for lunch before the afternoon lecture.

As he dressed, his thoughts drifted back over the past few days:
Alex's gradual but noticeable shift away from skepticism. Each
conversation felt like a puzzle piece falling into place, and that
day's lecture could possibly add another to the picture. Grabbing
his notepad, Sam headed out.

When he arrived at the café, Alex was already there. After
working their way through the seemingly endless buffet—soups,
salads, meats, fruits, and desserts—Sam grinned and said, "Ready
for a different kind of academic talk? This afternoon's lecture
is 'The Great Books of Antiquity: Their Legacy and Scientific

Reliability' with Professor Kendrick. I hear he'll be touching on Christian literature, including the Bible."

"This one should be interesting" Alex said. "Although I find it strange that the Bible gets lumped in with ancient literature like Homer or Plato."

Sam responded, "Why's that?"

Alex shrugged, saying, "I don't know . . . I've just heard the Bible is full of contradictions. And honestly, I thought the New Testament was written long after Jesus died—by guys who wanted to start a new religion. Seems more like legend than history."

Sam smiled. "That may not be the case. Let's listen to what the lecturer says.

Alex grinned. "Fair enough. Let's see what the old books have to say."

They quickly finished their meal and followed the flow of passengers into one of the ship's midsize auditoriums. People were already filing in, some chatting about how much they had enjoyed the lectures so far.

Sam and Alex spotted a few familiar faces from earlier talks. They found seats in the third row and settled in. Sam opened his notepad, ready to jot down relevant details from the presentation.

Precisely at two, a tall, bespectacled man in his late fifties stepped up to a podium on stage, tapping the microphone. He wore a casual blazer, his posture confident but approachable. The lights dimmed slightly, and a hush fell over the audience.

"Good morning, everyone," he began with a welcoming tone. "I'm Professor Andrew Kendrick, and it's my pleasure to talk to you about some of the greatest literary works that have shaped our understanding of the ancient world. We'll explore Greek and Roman classics, then shift gears to consider Hebrew and Christian writings—works that are often left out of 'great books' discussions but are undeniably influential. We'll close by examining how well these texts have been preserved and whether we can trust them as authentic records of the past."

Sam watched Alex lean forward, arms loosely crossed, curious to hear what the professor had to say. The professor's calm yet energized demeanor promised a thorough exploration rather than a cursory overview.

A slide appeared with a mosaic of ancient texts and busts of Greek and Roman thinkers.

"First," he began, "let's survey the Greek written works that have formed the backbone of Western thought. Before printing presses, before even bound books as we know them—these were the voices that shaped law, philosophy, literature, and ethics across centuries."

He paused, then gestured at a slide of an ancient scroll.

"We begin with Homer—the *Iliad* and the *Odyssey*. These epic poems weren't just literature; they were the moral and heroic frameworks for Greek identity. They gave structure to education and were recited in courts, classrooms, and around family hearths. In many ways, they were the Greek world's Bible before the Bible."

The slide changed to a profile of Plato, with excerpts from the *Republic*.

"Next, we come to Plato. His dialogues—especially the *Republic*—remain central to conversations on justice, governance, and the very nature of reality. Alongside Aristotle, whose *Nicomachean Ethics* and *Politics* laid the groundwork for logic and scientific inquiry, Plato's writings have influenced every era from the Roman Empire to Enlightenment Europe and into our modern political and academic institutions."

He clicked again, bringing up images of Herodotus and Thucydides.

"In terms of history, Herodotus and Thucydides gave the Western world two distinct models: one narrative and mythological, the other analytical and investigative. Without them, it's hard to imagine the development of historical thinking as we know it."

Next came Rome.

"With Virgil, especially the *Aeneid*, Rome forged a national epic rivaling Homer. And philosophers like Seneca, Marcus Aurelius, and Cicero provided a blueprint for Stoicism, law, and statesmanship—ideas that still echo in courtrooms and universities today."

He paused and folded his hands thoughtfully.

"These authors were not just literary figures. They were architects of worldview—builders of how civilizations would define virtue, law, reason, and meaning for generations to come."

Professor Kendrick paused briefly before continuing.

"Finally, let's consider what is arguably the most influential book in the history of Western civilization: the Bible—comprised of both the Old and New Testaments."

He gestured to a new slide that featured famous works of art, legal documents, and quotes from historical figures.

"From a literary perspective, the Bible has influenced more authors, more art, and more music than any other single work. But its contribution goes far deeper."

He clicked to another slide. "The Genesis account provided the foundation for a linear view of history—time with a beginning, a moral arc, and a purposeful end. This contrasts with the cyclical view common to many ancient religions."

Professor Kendrick continued. "From the Old Testament emerged not only Israel's religious tradition, but also its moral framework—rooted in covenant, law, and justice. The Ten Commandments laid the groundwork for moral responsibility, and biblical law undergirded many early legal systems in the West."

He then moved to a portrait of Jesus and the Sermon on the Mount.

"The New Testament introduced radical concepts that became the moral heartbeat of Western values: the dignity of the individual, the worth of the poor and marginalized, enemy-love, forgiveness, and sacrificial leadership. These were revolutionary in the Greco-Roman world."

A new image appeared showing the Magna Carta and early universities.

"It was the biblical view of a rational creator that helped launch the scientific revolution. The belief in an ordered universe governed by laws—observable and discoverable—found its roots not only in Aristotle, but also in Genesis."

He concluded the section with a final observation: "While Homer and Plato gave us epics and philosophy, the Bible gave us meaning, moral vision, and a redemptive narrative that has shaped human rights, charity, law, education, and the very concept of human equality. Whether you believe it to be divine or not, its influence is undeniable."

Professor Kendrick paused, then added: "If some of Jesus's teachings sound familiar today—like 'Love your neighbor as yourself' or 'Blessed are the meek'—it's because they've been echoing through Western culture for two thousand years."

He clicked to a slide quoting historian Tom Holland, author of *Dominion: How the Christian Revolution Remade the World*: "To live in a Western country is to live in a society still utterly saturated by Christian concepts and assumptions. The ethics of the Sermon on the Mount remain the hidden framework even of secular morality."

The professor looked toward the quote and said, "Even those who distance themselves from religion are often standing on moral ground that has been shaped, even unintentionally, by biblical roots."

He walked to the side of the podium and gestured to a new slide. It featured a table comparing manuscript counts and dates.

"Now, while these ancient works have had enormous influence, it's important to remember how fragile their transmission has been."

He pointed to the first row.

"Homer's *Iliad* is actually one of the best preserved texts from antiquity—yet even it survives in just under 650 manuscripts, the earliest of which dates nearly five hundred years after Homer is believed to have lived. For the *Odyssey*, the number is lower."

He advanced the slide.

"In the case of Plato—the man whose philosophy helped shape Western civilization—we have about seven to ten manuscripts of his major works, with the earliest copies appearing roughly twelve hundred years after he wrote them."

With a click, Plato's image was replaced by another ancient author.

"With Aristotle, whose logic and ethics are still taught today, we have fewer than fifty manuscripts, most from over a thousand years later. Herodotus and Thucydides, often called the fathers of history, are known to us through only eight or nine manuscripts each, with a time gap of more than thirteen hundred years between the originals and our earliest copies."

He paused to let the numbers settle in for the listeners.

"Now, none of this invalidates the content of these works. Scholars have reconstructed them with reasonable confidence. But it does illustrate the typical manuscript reality of ancient writings."

Professor Kendrick clicked to a new slide showing images of ancient scroll fragments nestled in desert caves. The title read, "The Dead Sea Scrolls: A Breakthrough in Biblical Scholarship."

He stepped forward, his voice taking on a tone of excitement.

"Up until the mid-twentieth century, critics of the Bible often claimed that the Old Testament had been hopelessly corrupted through generations of copying. They said, with some justification, that our earliest Hebrew manuscripts only dated back to around the tenth century AD—well over a thousand years after many of the original texts were written."

He paused to let that sink in.

"Then, in 1947, in a set of caves near the Dead Sea, Bedouin shepherds stumbled upon clay jars containing ancient scrolls—what we now call the Dead Sea Scrolls. What scholars discovered over the next few years would shake the academic world."

A new slide showed side-by-side comparisons of text fragments.

"Among the thousands of scrolls and fragments were copies of nearly every book of the Old Testament, some dating as early as the third century BC. Suddenly, we had manuscripts one thousand years older than the ones scholars had been relying on."

He let the room go quiet for a second.

"So, the natural question was: 'How different were they?' Had the text changed? The answer was extraordinary. Apart from minor variations—mostly spelling differences and copyist slips—the content of the biblical text had remained remarkably consistent."

Another slide highlighted the Book of Isaiah, one of the most complete scrolls found.

"For example, when comparing the Great Isaiah Scroll from Qumran with the Masoretic Text used in most Bibles today, scholars found that over 95 percent of the text was virtually identical. The few differences had no effect on doctrine or major themes."

He looked back at the audience.

"What the Dead Sea Scrolls confirmed was that the scribes who preserved these texts were incredibly meticulous. The Old Testament we hold in our hands today is not a distortion of the original, but a highly accurate transmission—carefully copied, carefully guarded. So, the next time someone claims the Bible was rewritten and corrupted over time, remember the caves of Qumran. We now know with confidence: The Old Testament hasn't changed nearly as much as many thought—it's been preserved."

Then the slide changed again. This time, a new bar chart emerged—one column towering far above the rest.

"Now let's talk about the New Testament."

He turned back to the audience.

"We have more than 5,800 Greek manuscripts of the New Testament. If you include early translations—Latin, Syriac, Coptic, Armenian—that number climbs to over 24,000 manuscript copies."

Murmurs stirred in the crowd.

"And the earliest fragment we possess—commonly referred to as 'P52,' a scrap from the Gospel of John—is dated to about 125 AD, only thirty to forty years after the original was likely written. That's astonishingly close in historical terms."

He advanced to a side-by-side comparison of all the works he'd mentioned.

"To put this in perspective: While other ancient documents have time gaps of eight hundred to thirteen hundred years between composition and earliest manuscript, the New Testament's gap is measured in decades. And the volume of manuscript evidence we have allows scholars to reconstruct the New Testament with over 99 percent textual accuracy."

Professor Kendrick faced the audience squarely.

"This doesn't prove the theological truth of the New Testament. But it does mean this: if we accept the writings of Plato, Homer, Herodotus, and Virgil based on manuscript evidence, we must at the very least grant that the New Testament is the most historically reliable document from the ancient world."

He let the final slide's quote rest for a few moments: "Historical reliability does not equal faith—but it may clear a path to consider it."

Sam and Alex joined the crowd slowly filtering out of the lecture hall, a hum of murmured conversations trailing behind.

Alex broke the silence. "Well . . . I wasn't expecting that." He exhaled and shook his head slightly. "I always thought the Bible was full of holes—rewritten over centuries like a myth evolving with the times. But . . . the manuscript evidence? That surprised me."

Sam gave a small nod, "Yeah, that part stunned me too when I first heard it. I grew up hearing the Bible was reliable, but I had no idea just how much more textual support it has compared to other ancient works."

"But doesn't that just mean we have a lot of early copies? I mean . . . that doesn't prove the content is true."

"You're right. Manuscript evidence doesn't prove it's true—but it does mean we're reading what they actually wrote, not some distorted version passed down like a game of telephone. And once you know that, you've got to decide what to do with the content itself."

Alex rubbed the back of his neck thoughtfully. "It's just . . . unsettling, honestly. I've always brushed off the Bible as folklore with a religious agenda. But if what we have is historically reliable—and if people like Paul were writing and dying for what they claimed to have seen—it's harder to just dismiss it as legend."

"Exactly. You don't have to believe it all at once. But you can at least take the next honest step and ask yourself: If it might be true . . . what would that mean for me?"

Alex chuckled. "You're good at that, you know—leaving me with uncomfortable but necessary questions."

Sam grinned. "That appears to be my role. But you're asking great questions and wrestling with what you're hearing. That says something."

> **QUESTION FOR REFLECTION:** *What difference would it make to you if the New Testament is not simply a religious book filled with beliefs, but a historically reliable account of real events that actually happened?*

CHAPTER 9

Jesus's Amazing Claims

O UTSIDE THE LECTURE hall, passengers lingered in small groups, conversing about Professor Kendrick's talk on the "Great Books of Antiquity."

"You know," Sam said thoughtfully, "the New Testament isn't just a collection of spiritual writings. It's a historical document—focused entirely on the person of Jesus: what he did, what he claimed, and what happened afterward."

Alex, ever the skeptic, crossed his arms. "I'll grant you the New Testament is impressive as an ancient manuscript. But how reliable is its portrayal of Jesus? People have been embellishing stories for centuries. That doesn't make them true. I mean, aren't all religions basically the same? From what I can tell, Jesus is just one more religious figure trying to help people live better lives."

Just then, a voice chimed in from behind them. "Pardon me—I couldn't help overhearing. You both raise important points. Allow me to introduce myself: Phillip Kellog, professor of comparative religion."

Sam extended his hand. "Nice to meet you. I'm Sam, and this is my friend Alex."

Phillip smiled warmly. "Pleasure to meet you both. I've been attending this Faith and Science cruise for years—such a fascinating blend of perspectives. In my experience, some of the best conversations happen after a good lecture."

"We were heading to the coffee bar to continue our discussion. Would you care to join us?" asked Sam.

"I would love to," said Phillip enthusiastically.

After they were seated and each had sipped their favorite coffee drink, Alex asked, "What's it like, teaching comparative religions? My take is that all religions say the same thing with slight variations. Would I be right?"

Phillip smiled. "That's a common assumption, but in reality, they are fundamentally different and only superficially similar. They all contain ethical teachings, some version of the Golden Rule, stories of redemption. But the deeper you go, the more different they become—especially when it comes to what they say about ultimate reality, the human condition, and how salvation is achieved."

"So, what does set them apart? And since we're on a faith-science cruise, how do they intersect with modern science?" Sam asked.

Phillip cradled his coffee mug. "Great question. To answer, I'll need to take you on a quick tour of the global religious landscape."

He leaned in, his voice thoughtful. "Take Hinduism, for instance. It envisions the universe as cyclical, governed by the eternal dance of Brahman—the impersonal, divine reality behind all things. Souls, or atmans, are caught in the cycle of samsara—birth, death, and rebirth—until they achieve moksha, or liberation. Now, while this framework is spiritually rich, it doesn't necessarily intersect with modern scientific understanding. The concept of karma influencing one's next life, for example, lies outside empirical verification. It's more metaphysical than testable.

"Buddhism arose partly as a reform movement within Hindu culture. It doesn't speak of a creator god and instead focuses on personal experience and the cessation of suffering. Its Four Noble Truths and the Eightfold Path are deeply psychological and ethical in nature. Interestingly, its emphasis on mindfulness and meditation has found empirical support in neuroscience. But again, core concepts like rebirth and nirvana, while central to the faith, fall outside the realm of scientific inquiry."

He took another sip of coffee, then continued. "Judaism stands on different ground. It's rooted in history and covenant. The God of the Hebrew Bible acts in time—delivering Israel from Egypt, giving the law, speaking through prophets. There's a historical claim being made, not just a metaphysical one. And while miracles aren't subject to scientific repeatability, Judaism nonetheless insists that God's actions took place in the observable world—in real locations, involving real people. The focus is on a chosen people, law, and justice—but still awaiting a messiah."

He gestured slightly. "Islam shares that emphasis on divine intervention in history. It claims that the Quran is the final and perfect revelation, dictated word for word by God through the prophet Muhammad. Like Judaism, it affirms a beginning to the universe, a creator, moral law, and accountability. However, the Quran is presented as timeless and unchangeable, which can create tension with scientific advances—such as in cosmology, biology, and even astronomy—depending on how literally certain passages are interpreted."

"Islam," he went on, "is very theistic—Allah is one, transcendent, utterly sovereign. Salvation comes through submission and obedience to God's will, expressed in the Quran and the teachings of Muhammad."

He looked at them both, pausing for effect. "Now, Christianity—this is where things really take a unique turn."

Alex raised an eyebrow. Sam leaned forward.

"Christianity," Phillip said, "makes a bold and unusual claim: that God became a man in a particular time and place. Not just that he acted in history, but that he *entered* it. Jesus of Nazareth, born under Roman rule, lived, taught, healed, was executed—and, his followers claim, rose from the dead. These are historical assertions, not abstract philosophies. They're subject to examination, corroboration, even skepticism. Christianity, more than any other faith, invites scrutiny."

He continued, raising a finger in emphasis. "And this is important: The Christian worldview gave rise to modern science. The early pioneers—Galileo, Kepler, Newton—believed the universe was orderly because it was created by a rational God. They expected laws of nature because they believed in a lawgiver. Christianity doesn't view faith and science as enemies, but as partners—two ways of knowing, grounded in the same reality.

"Here's where it gets interesting. Christianity isn't primarily about *what you do for God*. It's about what God has *done for you*. The New Testament doesn't just present Jesus as a wise teacher—it portrays him as the eternal Son of God who entered history, claimed to forgive sin, and rose from the dead."

Phillip looked thoughtfully at Alex. "You know, one of the most striking things when comparing religions is this: None of the major founders of world religions claimed to be God—except Jesus."

He held up an index finger to begin enumerating. "Take Buddha. He never claimed to be divine. In fact, he discouraged speculation about gods, focusing instead on the path to enlightenment through inner transformation."

He added a second finger. "Mohammed never claimed to be God. He insisted he was merely a prophet—*the* final prophet, yes—but still a servant delivering God's message, not God himself."

A third finger joined the other two. "Moses, central to Judaism, was a messenger and lawgiver, not divine. Even Hindu sages, while some are considered incarnations or avatars, never made exclusive claims to *be* the one true God over all creation."

He paused. "Jesus stands utterly alone in this regard. He didn't just point to truth—he claimed to *be* the truth. He didn't just teach the way to God—he said, 'I am the way, the truth, and the life. No one comes to the Father except through me.' That's not a prophet speaking. That's someone claiming exclusive divine authority."

Alex furrowed his brow. "But where else does he actually claim to be God? Some say that idea was just added later by his followers."

Phillip nodded. "That's a common misconception. But the Gospels—our earliest sources—contain multiple examples. In addition to John 8:58, where Jesus says, 'Before Abraham was, I am,' he also says in John 10:30, 'I and the Father are one.' The Jewish leaders immediately picked up stones to kill him—not for miscommunication, but for blasphemy, because he was making himself equal with God."

He continued, saying, "In Mark 14:61–62, at his trial before the high priest, Jesus is asked, 'Are you the Messiah, the Son of the Blessed One?' Jesus replies, 'I am, and you will see the Son of Man sitting at the right hand of the Mighty One and coming on the clouds of heaven.' That's a direct reference to Daniel 7, where the 'Son of Man' is a divine, heavenly figure who receives authority and worship. Again, the response? The high priest tears his robes and declares blasphemy. There's no ambiguity about what Jesus was claiming."

Sam nodded, adding, "And those claims were made in a context where such statements could get you executed."

Phillip leaned forward. "And again, this claim wasn't validated by words alone, but by what happened three days after he was executed—his resurrection. If he had stayed in the tomb, history might have forgotten him. But if he rose—as his followers and early eyewitnesses insisted—then his claim to divinity isn't just remarkable. It's true."

"Okay, I can accept that he lived," Alex admitted. "But being executed doesn't make someone divine."

"That's true, Alex," Sam responded, "but I believe the resurrection is what seals Jesus's claims. If that happened, then everything else changes."

"Exactly," Phillip continued. "The resurrection isn't presented as metaphor. Jesus died by Roman crucifixion. It's in all four Gospels but also mentioned by outside sources. The Jewish historian Josephus, who, in his writings, described Jesus's startling deeds and his crucifixion under Pilate, also references the claim that Jesus rose on the third day.

"The Romans were pros at execution—they wouldn't leave someone half dead. They speared him in the side to ensure he was gone, then buried him in a sealed tomb. Roman soldiers guarded that tomb. Yet by Sunday, it was open and empty. The earliest opponents of Christianity claimed the disciples stole the body. But these were the same disciples who ran for their lives when Jesus was arrested. They had zero motive—and no real ability to overcome armed soldiers.

"Some folks suggest he survived the cross—commonly called the 'swoon theory'—but that's pretty far-fetched. If he was half dead, battered, and wrapped in burial cloths, it's unlikely he could slip past Roman guards, appear to his frightened disciples, and motivate them to die for a lie."

He paused. "Plus, if the Jewish or Roman authorities wanted to squash the resurrection talk, all they had to do was show Jesus's dead body. That never happened, which strongly implies the body couldn't be produced."

"Finally," the professor concluded, "the disciples claimed to have seen Jesus alive over the next forty days. The apostle Paul wrote that Jesus appeared to over five hundred people at once. Sure, a hallucination might happen to an individual. But five hundred collectively? And these aren't gullible folks. Thomas doubted until he touched Jesus's wounds. The disciples had been terrified, but something flipped them from cowards to bold preachers who'd face martyrdom rather than recant their belief in Jesus's resurrection."

Alex exhaled. "That's a lot to consider."

Phillip paused reflectively, and then added, "C. S. Lewis wrote that if Jesus claimed to be God, we can't just label him a 'great moral teacher.' He'd either be lying, delusional, or telling the truth. Lewis wrote, 'Let's not come with any patronizing nonsense about his being a great human teacher. He hasn't left that open to us.'"

Sam added, "So, basically, Lewis is saying if Jesus made explicit claims to deity, we only have so many options: liar, lunatic, or Lord."

Alex cracked a faint, thoughtful smile. "A heavy statement."

Sam inclined his head. "Right. The big question is 'which?'"

"It does make you think," Alex acknowledged.

"Gentlemen," Phillip summed up, "I've studied world religions my entire life. They all have value, but none of them presents such a historical challenge as Christianity: a verifiable claim rooted in time and place."

Phillip glanced at his watch and smiled softly. "Well, I should let you both get on with your afternoon."

Sam stood and extended his hand. "Phillip, thank you. That was incredibly thought-provoking—especially the way you highlighted what sets Jesus apart from the other religious founders."

Alex nodded appreciatively. "Yes, I've never heard the uniqueness of Christianity laid out with such clarity. Really grateful you took the time to share that with us."

Phillip smiled warmly as he rose from the table. "It was my pleasure. These are the kinds of conversations that matter most—thoughtful, honest, and open. I'll let you two continue from here. Enjoy the rest of your cruise."

With a gentle nod, he turned and disappeared into the late afternoon crowd.

For a few moments, Sam and Alex sat quietly, sipping the last of their drinks, the sun casting long golden shadows across the deck.

Alex broke the silence. "He's sharp. I mean, I've heard people talk about world religions before, but this was different. Balanced . . . respectful . . . but still honest about the differences."

Sam looked over at him. "Yeah. I appreciated that too. Especially how he didn't try to pressure you—just presented the truth and left room for you to wrestle with it."

Alex exhaled slowly, gazing out at the horizon. "You know . . . if you'd asked me a year ago whether I'd ever be seriously considering the claims of Christianity, I would've laughed. But now?" He paused. "Now I'm not so sure. I'm not ready to jump in with both feet . . . but I can't ignore what I've heard either."

Sam smiled. "Sounds like one step closer."

Alex nodded. "Yeah. One step closer."

The wind picked up slightly as the ship glided forward, quiet except for the distant murmur of voices and clinking glasses. Two old friends sat side by side. Sam, already anchored in faith, wondered if Alex was beginning to drift toward an equally strong spiritual mooring.

QUESTION FOR REFLECTION: *If Jesus truly overcame death—rising from the grave as eyewitnesses claimed—what would that mean for his identity, his teachings, and his claim to be the messiah and the Son of God?*

CHAPTER 10

The Next Step

THE FINAL EVENING of the cruise had settled into a warm, quiet calm. The sun was dipping beneath the horizon, painting the ocean in streaks of amber and violet. Sam and Alex found a table in the café on the upper deck. They each settled in with a drink in hand.

Sam glanced over at Alex. "So . . . end of the cruise. A lot of miles traveled—and I'm not just talking about the sea. What are your thoughts?"

"You know, Sam . . . when this trip started, I came on as a skeptic. I started this cruise dead set on the idea that 'God' was just a crutch for people who couldn't face reality. I was just here for the scenery, the lectures, and maybe a break from work. But something changed."

He paused thoughtfully. "You know, it wasn't just one thing. Listening to the different speakers made me realize that my convictions about life weren't really built on a solid or informed foundation. They were scattered—like a puzzle dumped out on the table, all jumbled and upside down. But this week helped me start to put the pieces together. The picture's not fully clear yet, but for the first time, I feel like a pattern is beginning to emerge."

Alex exhaled before speaking again. "After Dr. Morgan's lectures on the laws of nature and the fine-tuned universe, it's hard to say the universe is here by accident. The statistical odds are so immense that chance becomes absurd. Then there was that conversation with Dr. Guillen about the universe's origin—how it might be more rational to believe in a creator than assume everything just popped out of nowhere."

Alex took another sip, then continued. "The biggest blow to my assumptions was Dr. Caldwell's insights on DNA. A sophisticated language inside every cell can't just evolve from chaos. Someone had to author that code. And Sara . . . well, she demolished my 'problem of pain and suffering' argument. She showed me it's possible God can still be good and powerful, even if suffering exists. She had a whole different framework—like a story that's not finished yet."

Sam nodded, listening quietly.

Alex went on. "And then the lecture on the Bible. I always thought it was just an old religious book, full of contradictions. But learning how well it's been preserved—how historically credible the New Testament documents are compared to other ancient texts—that challenged some assumptions I've held onto for years.

"But honestly, our time talking with Phillip had a particularly powerful impact on me. Not just how he explained the major religions—but how he showed that Jesus didn't just teach people to be good. He claimed to be God. And the New Testament presents him not as myth, but as a real, historical person who backed up his claims in a way no one else ever has."

Sam smiled. "That's a lot to take in."

Alex gave a slow, reflective smile. "I don't have all the answers . . . but I know this: I'm no longer an atheist. I believe there's a God. And I'm beginning to think he's not distant and disconnected from life on earth. And then Jesus. He adds an entirely new layer to the story. The more I learn about him, the more I'm drawn in."

Sam reached out and placed a hand on Alex's shoulder. "Alex, that's not a small shift—it's the start of something big."

"But I'm not sure what happens next. It's one thing to say, 'Yes, I believe in God,' but is it possible to actually know God? How does belief become personal, like it is for you?"

Sam turned towards Alex and said, "I can relate to what you're saying. Early in my faith journey I asked the same question. Someone showed me a simple diagram to help me understand how I could actually know God personally. Would you like me to share it with you?"

Alex responded intently, "Sure, I'd love to see it."

Sam picked up a napkin from the table, pulled out a pen and drew two horizontal lines "Let's say this top line represents God, and the bottom one represents man—humanity."

He tapped the upper line. "Let's start here—with God. Have you ever wondered how God sees us—his creation?"

Alex furrowed his brow. "That's a big question. The reality is I've never really thought about it."

Sam smiled. "Well, have you ever watched a football game and seen someone holding a sign that says 'John 3:16' in the end zone?"

Alex chuckled. "Yeah—usually right after a touchdown. I've always assumed it was a Bible verse, but I never knew what it meant."

"In fact, it's one of the most well-known verses in the Bible. It was written by one of Jesus's closest disciples and really sums up the heart of God."

Sam wrote "God's Love" along the top line and recited the verse:

"'For God so loved the world that He gave His only begotten Son, that whoever believes in Him shall not perish but have everlasting life.'

"God's not some distant, disconnected force. He created us to have a relationship—with him. Not necessarily a life without problems, but a life filled with meaning, peace, and purpose."

Alex nodded slowly. "Sara mentioned that. Even when she spoke about suffering, she described feeling God's presence. It's hard to explain away."

Sam smiled. "That's what the Bible shows over and over again—a God who cares deeply about individuals. Not just the world in general, but each person. That's the foundation: He wants us to *know* and *experience* his love."

Sam pointed to the bottom line on the napkin. "Let's talk about this line—us. See the space between the two lines? That gap represents the separation between God and humanity."

He looked at Alex and asked, "Why do you think that separation exists?"

Alex paused, thinking. "I'm not sure," he finally said. "I suspect it has something to do with us and not God. Maybe something we did. Am I close?

"Very close," Sam responded as he wrote on the lower line "Man's Sin." "Not just what we've done—but what we've *missed*. What comes to mind when you hear the word 'sin'?"

Alex gave a sheepish smile. "Honestly? All the things I like doing—but know I probably shouldn't."

Sam chuckled. "You're not alone. But here's something interesting—in the original Greek of the New Testament, the word for 'sin' literally means 'to miss the mark.' Like an archer aiming for the bullseye—and falling short."

Alex looked intrigued. "Missing the mark . . . so, not just rebellion, but failure to hit the target?"

Sam nodded. "Exactly. And that 'target' is God's perfect standard. Jesus described it as loving God with all your heart, soul, and mind—and loving your neighbor as yourself."

Alex exhaled. "That's a pretty high bar. Not much margin for messing up."

Sam smiled. "That's the whole point. The Bible says, 'For all have sinned and fall short of the glory of God.' And in another verse: 'For the wages of sin is death'—not just physical death, but spiritual separation from God."

He paused before continuing. "I used to think God graded on a curve. Like, as long as I wasn't as bad as some people, I was doing okay. But imagine we're all standing on a beach in California, and someone says, 'Let's have a swimming race.' I look around and see some people I can probably beat, so I'm thinking I might do okay. That's how some of us view our relationship with God: 'I'm certainly better than that person, so I should be okay with God.' Then we learn the race is to Hawaii! Some might go farther than others, but nobody's making it. That's how sin works—we all fall short."

Alex nodded slowly. "That really changes how I see it. We're all in the same boat."

"Exactly," Sam agreed. "And sin isn't just open rebellion. It can be passive indifference—just going through life saying, 'God, you may be there, but I'm going my own way.' Either way, it separates us from him."

Alex leaned in. "So, if we're separated like that—what's the solution?"

Sam's tone brightened. "That's where Jesus comes in. He didn't just teach the way back to God—he claimed to *be the way*. The bridge between a holy God and broken humanity."

He drew a vertical line from "God" to "Man" and wrote one more word: "Jesus."

Alex looked at it, his brow furrowed. "This is where Jesus comes into the story?"

Sam nodded. "Yes. God took the initiative and sent Jesus as his only provision for our sin. The apostle Paul, who used to persecute Christians, later wrote, 'God demonstrates His love for us in this: while we were still sinners, Christ died for us.' What do you think that means?"

Alex thought aloud, "It sounds like . . . God sent Jesus because he loved us. But why did Jesus have to *die?*"

"Good question," Sam said. "God isn't just loving—he's also just. And justice demands that wrongs be paid for. But instead of you or me paying the penalty, God provided the payment through his Son."

Sam continued. "Let me give you a picture. Imagine you're from a small town, and your dad is the local judge—respected, fair, known for justice. You come home from college for spring break, drink too much, and cause a major accident downtown. There are plenty of witnesses. You're clearly guilty."

Alex raised his eyebrows, picturing it.

"You're brought before your father in court," Sam went on. "He loves you—but he's also a just judge. The fine is way more than you can pay. So, what does he do? He steps down from the bench, walks over to your side, and pays the fine himself."

Alex nodded slowly. "So . . . Jesus paid the penalty I couldn't pay."

"Exactly," Sam said. "That's the heart of the first part of the gospel: Even though we're guilty, Christ died for us."

Alex looked up. "And the second part?"

"Jesus didn't stay dead," Sam said. "He rose again—conquering sin and death. His resurrection is what proves he wasn't just another teacher. He was who he claimed to be."

Alex sat back, absorbing it. "When Phillip talked about the historical Jesus, the part that stuck with me was that claim—that he rose from the dead."

Sam smiled. "That's the crux of it all. If Jesus rose from the dead, it validates everything he said. It means he truly *is* the bridge between us and God—spanning a gap we could never cross on our own."

Sam let the moment settle, then continued. "But here's something important to understand, Alex. What Jesus did—his death and resurrection—is God's gift to us. But like any gift, it's not yours until you personally receive it."

Sam watched Alex reflect, then added, "Remember our judge and his son who caused the accident?"

Alex nodded. "Sure. The son was guilty, but the father paid the fine."

Sam leaned in. "Right. But think about this: Even after the father steps down from the bench and offers to pay the penalty, the son still has a choice. He can accept the payment . . . or he can refuse it."

Alex looked up. "You mean, even if the judge loves him and pays the fine, the son's not free unless he accepts the gift?"

"Exactly," Sam said. "The father can offer the payment, but it doesn't become effective until the son says yes and takes it. The problem is, if the son doesn't accept the gift, the penalty won't be paid. That's how it works with Jesus too."

He continued. "Jesus already paid the full penalty for our sin. He died in our place—that part is done. But we each have to personally accept that gift. No one else can do it for us."

Alex leaned forward. "So how does someone actually do that?"

Sam reached again for his pen and added a small drawing of a door. "There's a powerful image in Revelation 3:20. It's where Jesus says, 'Here I am! I stand at the door and knock. If anyone hears my voice and opens the door, I will come in.' The picture here is of a door with no handle on the outside. The handle is only on the inside. Jesus doesn't force his way in."

Alex looked at the sketch. "So, the door represents . . . my heart?"

"Exactly," Sam confirmed, nodding. "He knocks—he invites—but it's up to each of us to open the door from the inside. That's what faith looks like: choosing to trust that God will do what he's promised. Receiving Christ means turning from running your own life and asking Jesus to come into your life—to forgive you and lead you. It's saying yes to him."

Alex looked down at the napkin again, then up at Sam. "That actually clears up a lot. I've been thinking it had to start with me being better. But maybe it starts with being honest. Tell me specifically, though: How would someone actually receive Christ? Like, what would they say or do?"

Sam nodded. "It's not about having the perfect words—it's about the posture of your heart. A simple prayer can express the desire of your heart to God."

He paused for a moment, then said, "When you are ready, it might sound something like this:

"'Jesus, I know I've sinned and been living life my own way. I believe you died on the cross for me and rose again. Right now, I open the door of my life to you. I ask you to forgive me, to come into my life, and to take control. I trust you and receive you as my Savior and Lord. Thank you for hearing my prayer. Amen.'"

Alex nodded slowly, still considering it. "That really helps . . . just hearing it said plainly. I'm not ready to pray right now, but I'm not brushing it off. I just want to be sure when I do pray, I *mean* it."

Sam smiled. "I respect that, Alex. God isn't rushing you. He knows when a heart is sincere, and he'll keep meeting you in the process. The important thing is you now know what it means and how to respond when that moment comes."

Alex nodded. "Yeah. I think so."

"A good next step might be to read the Gospel of John. Do you have a Bible at home?"

"Not really. My parents gave me one for high school graduation, but I have no clue where it is."

"How about I send you one?"

"I'd like that."

"When you get it, go to the fourth book in the New Testament. John was one of Jesus's closest disciples. He wrote his account with one clear purpose—to help people know who Jesus really is and to believe in him. It's personal, powerful, and full of insight into Jesus's heart."

"That sounds like something I need to do. Thanks, Sam, for everything. For not pushing—just listening and explaining."

Sam smiled. "You're welcome. And as you read John, just ask God to show himself to you. He loves answering that kind of prayer."

As they got up to leave, Sam asked Alex, "By the way—are you planning to go to homecoming this year?"

"I actually am. It will be fun to catch up with some old faces."

"Awesome—I'll be there too. Let's plan on connecting at the reunion."

Alex nodded, slipping the folded napkin into his jacket pocket. "Deal."

The two embraced. They walked out of the café to disembark from the ship and head for flights home—a new journey quietly underway.

> **QUESTION FOR REFLECTION:** *Why do you think knowing God through Christ is ultimately a matter of faith and trust rather than just learning and intellect?*

The Journey Continues

THE FALL AIR buzzed with energy as alumni gathered across the campus quad—laughing, hugging, and swapping stories. Sam scanned the crowd near the student union and smiled as he spotted a familiar face.

"Alex!" he called out.

Alex turned, grinning. "Sam! Man, it's good to see you."

They shared a quick embrace and stepped aside from the crowd, leaning against a brick wall with cups of coffee in hand.

Sam looked at Alex with a spark of anticipation. "How are you doing? Still working at the magazine?"

"I'm doing really good. And yes, still doing my journalism thing. My job's been redefined much more to my liking."

"That's great to hear. So, you told me back on the cruise you'd read the Gospel of John. What'd you think?"

Alex exhaled, a noticeable calm in his voice. "Honestly, Sam . . . it changed everything. I started reading it slowly, just like you said. At first, I was just trying to understand who Jesus was. But somewhere along the way—it got personal."

Sam nodded, listening.

Alex continued, "One night I was reading John 10, where Jesus says, 'I am the good shepherd.' I couldn't get past it. It hit me—he wasn't just a historical figure. He was pursuing *me*. So, I did it. I prayed. I invited him into my life like we talked about on the cruise."

Sam's face lit up. "That's wonderful, Alex."

Alex smiled as well. "Yeah . . . I can't fully explain it, but I've been experiencing a kind of peace I've never known before. Like I'm not alone anymore. His presence—it's real."

Sam placed a hand on his shoulder. "That's what he promises. I'm really excited for you, Alex. If your experience is like mine and many others that I know, you will look back on this as the most important decision you ever made."

Alex glanced around at the buzz of homecoming weekend. "If you had told me last year I'd be standing here talking about Jesus, peace, and faith—I would've laughed."

Sam grinned. "And yet, here you are . . . Here *we* are."

Alex chuckled. "Yeah. Here I am. And honestly . . . I've never felt more grounded."

Sam raised his coffee cup slightly. "To new life, and new beginnings."

They made their way over to a quieter bench beneath a big oak tree on the edge of campus. Students and alumni passed by, but the two friends were in their own moment.

"Would it be helpful if I shared a few things that have really helped me grow in my relationship with Christ?" asked Sam.

"You bet. Got another napkin sermon?" he added with a grin.

Sam laughed. "Not a napkin this time—but a word: growth. Easy to remember. After we receive Christ, our next step is to grow in him. It's like being born physically—no one says, 'Great, the baby's born, let's just leave him.' No—we nurture him, prepare him for this new world."

He continued, saying, "It's the same spiritually. You've stepped into a new kind of life, and now the goal is to grow. The Bible says we're to grow up into Christ, to become more like him. And here's what the acronym 'GROWTH' stands for:

"'G' is for 'going to God daily,' usually through a specific prayer time. I set aside some time each morning, sometimes just a few minutes, before I get into the hassle of the day. It's just talking with him honestly, like you would with someone who really cares. And it also means listening too—being still and paying attention to those gentle nudges or impressions God's spirit gives you.

"'R' is for 'reading God's Word daily.' The Bible is our food for growth. Having a set time each day where you can read God's Word is essential. It is like literally having God speak to you personally. I combine it with my prayer time in the morning. There are some great devotionals to help guide you in reading the Bible. Would you like me to text you an app that I use?"

"That would be great!" Alex said with enthusiasm.

"As I started reading the Bible," Sam continued, "one of the first verses I ever memorized was 1 John 5:11–13. It says: 'And this is the testimony: God has given us eternal life, and this life is in His Son. Whoever has the Son has life; whoever does not have the Son of God, does not have life. I write these things to you who believe in the name of the Son of God so that you may know that you have eternal life.'"

Sam paused and added, "That word 'know' really stuck with me. God doesn't want us living in doubt, wondering where we stand. If you've trusted Christ, he's in your life—and if he's in your life, then eternal life is yours. That assurance isn't based on how you feel day to day—it's based on God's promise."

Alex nodded. "So, the confidence comes from his Word, not my emotions."

Sam smiled and said, "You got it!"

He continued with the acronym. "The next letter is 'O' for 'obeying what you learn.' As you read the Bible, you'll start to see how God wants you to live, respond, and love. And the challenge is to obey. I once heard about a young man in a remote village church who used to leave every sermon early. The pastor finally asked why, and the young man said, 'I stay until I hear something I should do. Then I leave to go do it.' That's the idea. Don't just learn—*live* it."

Alex laughed. "I like that. Straight to the point."

"'W,'" Sam continued, "is for 'witnessing.' When I say 'witnessing,' what comes to your mind?"

Alex sat back. "Something a little intrusive. The witnesses I've encountered have been dressed in suits, knocking on doors."

Sam laughed. "I would agree, not very attractive. The Bible describes witnessing as sharing with others what we have experienced in our relationship with Christ. We're Christ's representatives. Being a witness also doesn't mean having all the answers—it just means sharing what Jesus has done in your life and encouraging others to explore it for themselves."

Sam leaned in then and said, "Alex, wouldn't it be weird if we kept quiet about the most important thing ever to happen to us?"

Alex smiled, replying, "Yeah, I guess it would. I'm not sure exactly what I would say, but I get the idea."

Sam returned to the acronym. "'T' is for 'time with believers.' Other believers can be a vital source of encouragement, support, and accountability as you grow in your relationship with Christ. They can pray with you, answer questions, and walk alongside you during challenging times. Sharing life together helps you stay grounded and reminds you that you're not alone on this journey.

"'H,' finally, refers to the Holy Spirit. When you accept Christ, the Holy Spirit comes to live within you. He works in your heart, changing your desires and helping you become the person God created you to be. The Holy Spirit gives you the power to live out the Christian life—not in your own strength, but in his. As you learn to listen to him and follow his lead, he produces the qualities of Christ—like love, joy, peace, patience, and kindness—throughout your life."

Sam paused, letting the whole picture settle in before continuing. "Growing in your faith is about walking daily with Jesus. Spending time with him in prayer and Scripture. Letting him shape your thinking, your decisions, your relationships. Sharing him with others. It's not about perfection—it's about availability."

Sam added thoughtfully, "And one more very important thing—Christianity isn't a solo sport. God designed us to grow in community. Assignment number one is to find a church that teaches the Bible and helps people grow in their faith."

Alex responded quickly, saying, "I know a couple of guys at work who are involved in a church I've heard some good things about. I'll check with them."

"That's a good next step."

They both grew quiet, the weight of this new chapter settling over them. After a moment, Alex cleared his throat.

"You know, if you hadn't been so patient—on the cruise and after—I don't think I'd be here right now."

Sam looked at him with kind eyes. "Hey, it's been a blessing just to walk with you. Honestly, I'm just grateful God let me play a small part in something this big. He's the one who's been drawing you the whole time."

They chatted a while longer about work, life, and little moments that now felt richer in light of this spiritual journey. Eventually, they stood to say goodbye.

Sam gave Alex a hug. "I'm just a phone call away. Let's plan to catch up next month and see how things are going, okay?"

Alex nodded, smiling. "Absolutely. I'd like that."

As Sam walked back across the quad, watching the golden leaves swirl around his feet, he couldn't help but smile. God had used his availability on the cruise, simple conversations, shared coffees, and a few drawings on a napkin to help open someone's heart to a new life. And now his friend Alex was walking forward—into a journey only just beginning.

ABOUT THE AUTHOR |

Bruce Cook is a graduate of the Georgia Institute of Technology, where he earned a degree in industrial engineering, and of Harvard Business School, where he received his MBA. While at Harvard, Bruce was challenged to consider the claims of Christ and moved from skepticism to faith. During his final year, he and three classmates wrote their graduate research paper on Campus Crusade for Christ (Cru), an organization they were actively involved in. Upon graduation, Bruce joined Cru, serving as assistant to its founder and president to help implement their research recommendations. He later became national director of *Here's Life America*.

Bruce went on to found and lead Leadership Dynamics International, a Christian leadership training organization that integrated biblical principles with proven management practices. Through seminars conducted across North America, Europe, Asia, and Latin America, the ministry equipped thousands of Christian leaders for greater impact.

In addition to ministry and leadership development, Bruce has been active in Georgia state government and civic affairs. He has served by gubernatorial appointment on the boards of the Georgia Department of Human Resources, the Department of Community Affairs, and the Commission for a New Georgia.

Bruce has also held CEO roles in the health care and education sectors. He is the author of three books and has been featured in interviews on CNN, *CBS Evening News*, *ABC News*, and the *Wall Street Journal Radio Network*.

He and his wife, Donna, live in Atlanta. They are the proud parents of two grown children and grandparents of four.

REFERENCES FOR FURTHER STUDY |

CHAPTER 2: WHO WROTE THE LAWS?

1. Flew, Anthony. *There Is a God: How the World's Most Notorious Atheist Changed His Mind.* HarperOne, 2008.

2. The Laws of Thermodynamics
   - Physics and Astronomy Online. "What is a simple definition of the laws of thermodynamics?" PhysLink. Accessed April 20, 2024. https://www.physlink.com/education/askexperts/ae_thermo.cfm.
   - Atkins, P. The Laws of Thermodynamics: A Very Short Introduction, Oxford University Press, 2010.
   - Tipler, P., & Mosca, G. *Physics for Scientists and Engineers*, W.H. Freeman & Co., 2007, Sections on Thermodynamics

3. Newton's Laws of Motion and Universal Gravitation
   - *National Geographic. "Isaac Newton: Who He Was, Why Apples Are Falling."* Accessed May 20,2024. https://education.nationalgeographic.org/resource/isaac-newton-who-he-was-why-apples-are-falling/.
   - Newton, Isaac. *The Principia: Mathematical Principles of Natural Philosophy.* Translated by I. Bernard Cohen and Anne Whitman. University of California Press, 1999.
     o For a good modern summary: Hawking, Stephen. "Chapter 3: The Expanding Universe." In A *Brief History of Time.* Bantam Books, 1988.

4. Einstein on the Cosmic Order and God
   - Albert Einstein is often quoted as saying, "The most incomprehensible thing about the universe is that it is comprehensible."

- Source: Einstein, Albert. "Physics and Reality." *Journal of the Franklin Institute* 221, no. 3 (1936): 349–82. https://doi.org/10.1016/S0016-0032(36)91047-5.

- Einstein also wrote the following in a 1936 letter to a child who asked him if scientists pray: "Everyone who is seriously involved in the pursuit of science becomes convinced that a spirit is manifest in the laws of the Universe—a spirit vastly superior to that of man."
  - Source: Isaacson, Walter. *Einstein: His Life and Universe.* Simon & Schuster, 2007.

5. Newton's View of Gravity as the Hand of God
   - Newton wrote in the "General Scholium" to the *Principia*: "This most beautiful system of the sun, planets, and comets could only proceed from the counsel and dominion of an intelligent and powerful Being."
     - Newton, Isaac. *The Principia: Mathematical Principles of Natural Philosophy.* Translated by I. Bernard Cohen and Anne Whitman. University of California Press, 1999. See page 943.

6. Darwin on the Impossibility of Blind Chance
   - In an 1860 letter to Asa Gray, Darwin wrote, "The impossibility of conceiving that this grand and wondrous universe, with our conscious selves, arose through chance, seems to me the chief argument for the existence of God."
     - Source: Darwin, Charles. Charles Darwin to Asa Gray, May 22, 1860. Darwin Correspondence Project. https://www.darwinproject.ac.uk/letter/?docId=letters/DCP-LETT-2814.xml.

ADDITIONAL SUGGESTED READING

- Lennox, John C. *God's Undertaker: Has Science Buried God?* Lion Hudson, 2009.
- Polkinghorne, John C. *Science and Providence: God's Interaction with the World.* Templeton Foundation Press, 2005.
- Davies, Paul. *The Mind of God: The Scientific Basis for a Rational World.* Simon & Schuster, 1992.

CHAPTER 3: IN THE BEGINNING

1. Gamow, George. *My World Line: An Informal Autobiography*. Viking Press, 1970. See page 44.

2. Strobel, Lee. *Is God Real? Exploring the Ultimate Question of Life*. Zondervan Books, 2023. See page 27.

3. Guillen, Michael. *Believing Is Seeing*. Tyndale, 2021. See pages 16, 35,147–148.

4. Boa, Kenneth D. and Robert M. Bowman Jr. *20 Compelling Evidences That God Exists*. David C Cook, 2005. See page 38.

5. Funk, Cary and Lee Rainey. "Public and Scientists' Views on Science and Society." Pew Research Center, January 29, 2015. https://www.pewresearch.org/science/2015/01/29/public-and-scientists-views-on-science-and-society/.

6. The Size and Vastness of the Universe
   - Tyson, Neil deGrasse. *Astrophysics for People in a Hurry*. W.W. Norton, 2017.
   - Adams, Fred. *Origins of Existence: How Life Emerged in the Universe*. Free Press, 2002.

7. Einstein's Cosmological Constant ("Biggest Blunder")
   - Gamow. *My World Line: An Informal Autobiography*.
     o Gamow recounts Einstein's later reference to the cosmological constant as his "biggest blunder."
   - Isaacson. *Einstein: His Life and Universe*.

8. Hubble's Discovery of the Expanding Universe
   - Hubble, Edwin. "A Relation Between Distance and Radial Velocity Among Extra-Galactic Nebulae." *Proceedings of the National Academy of Sciences of the United States of America* 15, no. 8, (1929): 168–173. https://doi.org/10.1073/pnas.15.3.1.
   - Bartusiak, Marcia. *The Day We Found the Universe*. Pantheon, 2009.

9. The Universe Had a Beginning (Big Bang Theory)
   - Lemaître, Georges. "A Homogeneous Universe of Constant Mass and Increasing Radius Accounting for the Radial Velocity of Extra-Galactic Nebulae." *Monthly Notices of the Royal Astronomical Society* 91, no. 5 (1931): 483–490. https://doi.org/10.1093/mnras/91.5.483.
   - Kragh, Helge. *Cosmology and Controversy: The Historical Development of Two Theories of the Universe*. Princeton University Press, 1996.

10. Bell Labs Discovery of Cosmic Microwave Background Radiation
    • Penzias, Arno A., and Robert W. Wilson. "A Measurement of Excess Antenna Temperature at 4080 Mc/s." *Astrophysical Journal* 142 (1965): 419–421. https://adsabs.harvard.edu/full/1965ApJ...142..419P.
    • Overbye, Dennis. *Lonely Hearts of the Cosmos.* Back Bay Books, 1999.

11. NASA COBE Satellite Confirmation
    • Smoot, George, and Keay Davidson. *Wrinkles in Time: The Imprint of Creation.* Little, Brown, 1993.
    • COBE mission summary: National Aeronautics and Space Administration Goddard Space Flight Center. "Cosmic Background Explorer (COBE)." Accessed July 15, 2025. https://lambda.gsfc.nasa.gov/product/cobe/.

12. Quantum Vacuum Theory
    • Vilenkin, Alex. *Many Worlds in One: The Search for Other Universes.* Hill and Wang, 2006.
    • Davies, Paul. *The Goldilocks Enigma: Why Is the Universe Just Right for Life?* Allen Lane, 2006.

13. Hawking's Arguments on Gravity and Spontaneous Creation
    • Hawking, Stephen, and Leonard Mlodinow. *The Grand Design.* Bantam, 2010. See page 180.
        ○ Hawking argued, "Because there is a law such as gravity, the universe can and will create itself from nothing."
    • Ellis, George F.R., et al. "Multiverses and Physical Cosmology." *Monthly Notices of the Royal Astronomical Society* 347, no. 3 (2014): 921–936. https://doi.org/10.1111/j.1365-2966.2004.07261.x.
        ○ A scientific critique of some of Hawking's cosmological arguments.

14. Where Did the Big Bang Come From?
    • Guth, Alan. *The Inflationary Universe: The Quest for a New Theory of Cosmic Origins.* Perseus Books, 1997.
    • Krauss, Lawrence M. *A Universe from Nothing: Why There Is Something Rather than Nothing.* Free Press, 2012.

ADDITIONAL SUGGESTED READING

• Lennox, John. *God and Stephen Hawking: Whose Design Is It Anyway?* Lion Books, 2011.
• Craig, William Lane. *Reasonable Faith: Christian Truth and Apologetics,* 3rd ed. Crossway, 2008. See especially Chapter 3 on cosmology.

CHAPTER 4: HOW THE EARTH GOT JUST RIGHT

1. Carter, Brandon. "Large Number Coincidences and the Anthropic Principle in Cosmology." In *International Astronomical Union Symposium No. 63: Confrontation of Cosmological Theories with Observational Data*, edited by M.S. Longair (D. Reidel, 1973).

2. Ross, Hugh. *Why the Universe Is the Way It Is.* Baker Books, 2008.

3. Hedin, Eric. *Canceled Science.* Discovery Institute Press, 2021. See page 65.

4. Hawking. *A Brief History of Time.* See page 128.

5. Davies. *The Goldilocks Enigma.*

6. Flew. *There Is a God.* See page 119.

7. Drake, Nadia. "What Is the Multiverse—and Is There Any Evidence It Really Exists?" *National Geographic.* March 13, 2023. https://www.nationalgeographic.com/science/article/what-is-the-multiverse.

8. Boa and Bowman Jr. *20 Compelling Evidences That God Exists.* See pages 42–43.

9. The Fine-Tuning of the Universe
   - Barrow, John D., and Frank J. Tipler. *The Anthropic Cosmological Principle.* Oxford University Press, 1986.
   - Rees, Martin. *Just Six Numbers: The Deep Forces That Shape the Universe.* Basic Books, 2000.
   - Collins, Robin. "The Teleological Argument: An Exploration of the Fine-Tuning of the Universe." In *The Blackwell Companion to Natural Theology*, edited by William Lane Craig and J.P. Moreland. Wiley-Blackwell, 2012.

10. The Anthropic Principle
    - Carter. "Large Number Coincidences and the Anthropic Principle in Cosmology."
    - Davies. *The Goldilocks Enigma.*

11. Earth's Unique Habitability Factors
    - Ward, Peter D., and Donald Brownlee. *Rare Earth: Why Complex Life Is Uncommon in the Universe.* Copernicus, 2000.
      - Classic work arguing Earth's combination of conditions may be extremely rare.
    - Gonzalez, Guillermo, and Jay W. Richards. *The Privileged Planet: How Our Place in the Cosmos Is Designed for Discovery.* Regnery Publishing, 2004.

12. Key Fine-Tuning Examples
    - Location in the galaxy: Ward and Brownlee, *Rare Earth.*

- Stable Sun: Rees, *Just Six Numbers.*
- Right atmosphere, magnetic field, plate tectonics, and water balance: Gonzalez and Richards, *The Privileged Planet.*
- Gravitational constant, strong and weak nuclear force, cosmological constant: Barrow and Tipler, *Anthropic Cosmological Principle.*

13. Improbabilities of Chance-Only Explanations
   - Hoyle, Fred, and Chandra Wickramasinghe. *Evolution from Space: A Theory of Cosmic Creationism.* Simon & Schuster, 1982. See page 130.
      o Includes famous Hoyle quote which likens chance-formation of life to a tornado assembling a 747 in a junkyard.
   - Meyer, Stephen C. *The Return of the God Hypothesis: Three Scientific Discoveries That Reveal the Mind Behind the Universe.* HarperOne, 2021.

14. Critiques of Naturalist Explanations
   - Lennox, John. *God's Undertaker: Has Science Buried God?* Lion Hudson, 2009.
   - Craig, William Lane. *On Guard: Defending Your Faith with Reason and Precision.* David C. Cook, 2010.

ADDITIONAL SUGGESTED READING
- Strobel, Lee. *The Case for a Creator.* Zondervan, 2004.
- Axe, Douglas. *Undeniable: How Biology Confirms Our Intuition That Life Is Designed.* HarperOne, 2016.

CHAPTER 5: WHO WROTE THE DNA CODE?

1. Flew. *There is A God*. See pages 75–76.

2. Alberts, Bruce. "The Cell as a Collection of Protein Machines," *Cell* 92, no. 3 (1998): 291–294.

3. Strobel. *The Case for a Creator*. See pages 220–225.

4. "Millier-Urey Experiment." *Encyclopedia Britannica*. Accessed July 27, 2025. www.britannica.com/print/article/1402808.

5. Boa and Bowman. *20 Compelling Evidences That God Exists*. See page 56.

6. Geisler, Norman L. *How to Know God Exists: Scientific Proof of God*. Harvest House Publishers, 2008. See pages 131, 165.

7. Guillen. *Believing Is Seeing*. See page 150.

8. Origin of Life and DNA Complexity
   - Meyer, Stephen C. *Signature in the Cell: DNA and the Evidence for Intelligent Design*. HarperOne, 2009.
   - Davies, Paul. *The Fifth Miracle: The Search for the Origin and Meaning of Life*. Simon & Schuster, 1999.
   - Koonin, Eugene V. *The Logic of Chance: The Nature and Origin of Biological Evolution*. FT Press, 2011.

9. The Discovery of DNA Structure
   - Watson, James D., and Francis H.C. Crick. "Molecular Structure of Nucleic Acids: A Structure for Deoxyribose Nucleic Acid." *Nature* 171 (1953): 737–738.
   - Watson, James D. *The Double Helix: A Personal Account of the Discovery of the Structure of DNA*. Atheneum, 1968.

10. The Digital Information in DNA
    - Meyer, Stephen C. *Signature in the Cell: DNA and the Evidence for Intelligent Design*. HarperOne, 2009.
    - Yockey, Hubert P. *Information Theory, Evolution, and the Origin of Life*. Cambridge University Press, 2005.

11. The Complexity and Specificity of DNA
    - Axe. *Undeniable*.
    - Denton, Michael. *Evolution: A Theory in Crisis*. Adler & Adler, 1986.
    - Denton, Michael. *The Miracle of the Cell*. Discovery Institute Press, 2020.

12. The Improbability of Life by Random Chance
    - Hoyle. *The Intelligent Universe*.
    - Meyer. *The Return of the God Hypothesis*.

13. Origin of the Genetic Code: Naturalism Versus Design
    - Koonin. *The Logic of Chance.*
    - Davies. *The Fifth Miracle.*
    - Shapiro, Robert. *Origins: A Skeptic's Guide to the Creation of Life on Earth.* Summit Books, 1986.

14. The Argument for Intelligent Design in Information Systems
    - Dembski, William A. *The Design Inference: Eliminating Chance Through Small Probabilities.* Cambridge University Press, 1998.
    - Meyer. *Signature in the Cell.* Meyer's book is the central work on this subject.

15. Critiques and Counterarguments
    - Dawkins, Richard. *The Blind Watchmaker: Why the Evidence of Evolution Reveals a Universe Without Design.* W.W. Norton & Co., 1986.
    - Coyne, Jerry A. *Why Evolution Is True.* Viking, 2009.

ADDITIONAL SUGGESTED READING
- Strobel. *The Case for a Creator.*
- Behe, Michael J. *Darwin's Black Box: The Biochemical Challenge to Evolution.* Free Press, 1996.
- Behe, Michael J. *The Edge of Evolution: The Search for the Limits of Darwinism.* Free Press, 2007.

CHAPTER 6: WHERE CONSCIOUSNESS RESIDES

1. Greyson, Bruce. *After: A Doctor Explores What Near-Death Experiences Reveal About Life and Beyond.* St. Martin's Essentials, 2021.

2. Chesterton, G.K. *The Everlasting Man.* Ignatius Press, 1993.

3. Penfield, Wilder. *The Mystery of the Mind: A Critical Study of Consciousness and the Human Brain.* Princeton University Press, 1975.

4. Neal, Mary C. *To Heaven and Back: A Doctor's Extraordinary Account of Her Death, Heaven, Angels, and Life Again.* WaterBrook Press, 2011.

5. Noë, Alva. *Out of Our Heads: Why You Are Not Your Brain, and Other Lessons from the Biology of Consciousness.* Hill and Wang, 2009.

6. Herbert, Nick. *Elemental Mind: Human Consciousness and the New Physics.* Dutton, 1993.

7. Guillen, Michael. *Amazing Truths: How Science and the Bible Agree.* HarperOne, 2016. See page 61.

8. Hedin, Eric. *Canceled Science: What Some Atheists Don't Want You to See.* Discovery Institute Press, 2021. See page 194.

9. The Mind-Body Problem: Is the Brain the Same as the Mind?
   - Chalmers, David J. *The Conscious Mind: In Search of a Fundamental Theory.* Oxford University Press, 1996.
   - Searle, John R. *The Mystery of Consciousness.* New York Review of Books, 1997.
   - Nagel, Thomas. *Mind and Cosmos: Why the Materialist Neo-Darwinian Conception of Nature Is Almost Certainly False.* Oxford University Press, 2012.

10. The Hard Problem of Consciousness
    - Chalmers, David J. "Facing Up to the Problem of Consciousness." *Journal of Consciousness Studies* 2, no. 3 (1995): 200–219.
    - Goff, Philip. *Galileo's Error: Foundations for a New Science of Consciousness.* Pantheon, 2019.

11. The Immaterial Self and Free Will
    - Libet, Benjamin. *Mind Time: The Temporal Factor in Consciousness*. Harvard University Press, 2004.
        o Includes Libet's experiments on readiness potentials and voluntary action.
    - Moreland, J.P. *The Recalcitrant* Imago Dei: *Human Persons and the Failure of Naturalism*. SCM Press, 2009.

12. Materialism Versus Dualism
    - Dennett, Daniel C. *Consciousness Explained*. Little, Brown and Co., 1991.
        o A naturalist/materialist perspective on consciousness.
    - Moreland, J.P., and Scott Rae. *Body and Soul: Human Nature and the Crisis in Ethics*. InterVarsity Press, 2000.
    - Swinburne, Richard. *The Evolution of the Soul*. Oxford University Press, 1997.

13. The Argument for the Soul
    - Moreland, J.P., and William Lane Craig. *Philosophical Foundations for a Christian Worldview*. IVP Academic, 2003.
    - Meyer. *The Return of the God Hypothesis*. See Chapter 19: "The Mystery of Consciousness."

14. Near-Death Experiences
    - Sabom, Michael. *Light and Death: One Doctor's Fascinating Account of Near-Death Experiences*. Zondervan, 1998.
    - Long, Jeffrey. *Evidence of the Afterlife: The Science of Near-Death Experiences*. HarperOne, 2010.
    - Greyson, Bruce. *After.*

ADDITIONAL SUGGESTED READING
- Strobel. *The Case for a Creator*. See Chapter 10: "The Evidence of Consciousness: The Enigma of the Mind."
- D'Souza, Dinesh. *Life After Death: The Evidence*. Regnery Publishing, 2009.

CHAPTER 7: WHY PAIN AND SUFFERING?

1. Wolf, Katherine. *Treasures in the Dark: 90 Reflections on Finding Bright Hope Hidden in the Hurting.* W Publishing Group, 2024.

2. Eareckson Tada, Joni. "Overcoming the Unthinkable with Joni Eareckson Tada." Interview. Wonderfully Made, April 25, 2022. https://wonderfullymade.org/2022/04/25/overcoming-the-unthinkable-with-joni-eareckson-tada/.

3. Cru. "Why Does God Allow Suffering?" Accessed July 16, 2025. https://www.cru.org/us/en/train-and-grow/life-and-relationships/hardships/why-does-god-allow-suffering.html.

4. Lewis, C. S. *Mere Christianity.* HarperOne, 2001. See discussion of the moral law argument, pages 3–32.

5. Etheredge, Craig. "If God Is Good, Why Does God Allow Suffering?" Discipleship.org. Accessed July 16, 2025. https://discipleship.org/blog/if-god-is-good-why-does-god-allow/.

6. Strobel. *Is God Real?* See page 149.

7. The Problem of Evil
   - Mackie, J.L. "Evil and Omnipotence." *Mind* 64, no. 254 (1955): 200–212.
     o Classic philosophical formulation of the logical problem of evil.
   - Rowe, William L. "The Problem of Evil and Some Varieties of Atheism." *American Philosophical Quarterly* 16, no. 4 (1979): 335–341.

8. Christian Responses to the Problem of Evil
   - Plantinga, Alvin. *God, Freedom, and Evil.* William B. Eerdmans, 1974.
     o Groundbreaking treatise on the free-will defense.
   - Moreland and Craig. *Philosophical Foundations for a Christian Worldview.*
     o See excellent chapters on evil and suffering.

9. Suffering as Part of a Broken Creation
   - Lewis, C. S. *The Problem of Pain.* HarperOne, 2015.
     o Classic Christian explanation of why a good God allows pain.
   - Keller, Timothy. *Walking with God Through Pain and Suffering.* Dutton, 2013.

10. God's Identification with Suffering
    - Stott, John. *The Cross of Christ.* InterVarsity Press, 1986.

      o Profound reflection on God's entry into suffering through Jesus.
- Volf, Miroslav. *Exclusion and Embrace: A Theological Exploration of Identity, Otherness, and Reconciliation.* Abingdon Press, 1996.

11. Redemptive Purpose in Suffering
- Guinness, Os. *Unspeakable: Facing Up to Evil in an Age of Genocide and Terror.* HarperOne, 2005.
- Wright, N.T. *Evil and the Justice of God.* InterVarsity Press, 2006.

12. Existential and Emotional Aspect of Suffering
- Yancey, Philip. *Where Is God When It Hurts?* Zondervan, 1977.
- Lewis, C. S. *A Grief Observed.* HarperOne, 2015.

13. Atheist Arguments for Evil
- Harris, Sam. *The End of Faith: Religion, Terror, and the Future of Reason.* W.W. Norton, 2004. See Chapter 6: "A Science of Good and Evil."
- Hitchens, Christopher. *God Is Not Great: How Religion Poisons Everything.* Twelve Books, 2007.

ADDITIONAL SUGGESTED READING
- Lennox, John. *Where Is God in a Coronavirus World?* The Good Book Company, 2020.
- Craig. *On Guard.* See Chapter 6: "Can We Be Good Without God?".

CHAPTER 8: IS THE BIBLE RELIABLE?

1. The Manuscript Evidence of the New Testament
   - Metzger, Bruce M. and Bart D. Ehrman. *The Text of the New Testament: Its Transmission, Corruption, and Restoration*, 4th Edition. Oxford University Press, 2005.
   - Bruce, F.F. *The New Testament Documents: Are They Reliable?* William B. Eerdmans/InterVarsity Press, 2003. Originally published in 1943; still a classic.
   - Wallace, Daniel B., ed. *Revisiting the Corruption of the New Testament: Manuscript, Patristic, and Apocryphal Evidence.* Kregel, 2011.

2. Comparison with Other Ancient Texts
   - Geisler, Norman L., and William E. Nix. *A General Introduction to the Bible: Revised and Expanded.* Moody Press, 1986. See chapters on manuscript comparisons.
   - McDowell, Josh and Sean McDowell. *Evidence That Demands a Verdict: Life-Changing Truth for a Skeptical World*, Updated Edition. Thomas Nelson, 2017.
     - o Includes excellent charts comparing New Testament manuscripts with Homer, Plato, Caesar, etc.

3. The Dead Sea Scrolls and Old Testament Reliability
   - VanderKam, James, and Peter Flint. *The Meaning of the Dead Sea Scrolls: Their Significance for Understanding the Bible, Judaism, Jesus, and Christianity.* HarperSanFrancisco, 2002.
   - Burrows, Millar. *The Dead Sea Scrolls.* Viking Press, 1955.
   - Evans, Craig A. *Jesus and the Manuscripts: What We Can Learn from the Oldest Texts.* Hendrickson Academic, 2020.

4. Early Dating of the New Testament
   - Blomberg, Craig L. *The Historical Reliability of the New Testament: Countering the Challenges to Evangelical Christian Beliefs.* B&H Academic, 2016.
   - Bauckham, Richard. *Jesus and the Eyewitnesses: The Gospels as Eyewitness Testimony.* William B. Eerdmans, 2006.
   - Robinson, John A.T. *Redating the New Testament.* Westminster Press, 1976.

5. Eyewitness Testimony and Oral Tradition
   - Bauckham. *Jesus and the Eyewitnesses.*
   - Keener, Craig S. *Christobiography: Memory, History, and the Reliability of the Gospels.* William B. Eerdmans, 2019.

6. Archaeological Support for Biblical Accuracy

- Price, Randall. *The Stones Cry Out: What Archaeology Reveals About the Truth of the Bible*. Harvest House, 1997.
- Yamauchi, Edwin. *The Stones and the Scriptures*. Holman, 1972.
- Hoffmeier, James K. *The Archaeology of the Bible*. Lion Hudson, 2008.

7. Non-Christian Sources Corroborating the New Testament
- Habermas, Gary R. *The Historical Jesus: Ancient Evidence for the Life of Christ*. College Press, 1996.
- Tacitus. *Annals* XV.44.
- Josephus. *Antiquities of the Jews* XVIII.3.

8. Transmission Accuracy and Scribe Practices
- Tov, Emanuel. *Textual Criticism of the Hebrew Bible*. Fortress Press, 2001.
- Greenlee, J. Harold. *Introduction to New Testament Textual Criticism*. Hendrickson Publishers, 1995.

ADDITIONAL SUGGESTED READING

- Strobel, Lee. *The Case for Christ*. Zondervan, 1998.
- Wright, N.T. *The New Testament and the People of God*. Fortress Press, 1992.
- Evans, Craig A. *Fabricating Jesus: How Modern Scholars Distort the Gospels*. InterVarsity Press, 2006.

CHAPTER 9: JESUS'S AMAZING CLAIMS

1. The Historical Jesus: Existence and Sources
   - Habermas, Gary R., and Michael R. Licona. *The Case for the Resurrection of Jesus.* Kregel, 2004.
   - Craig, William Lane. *Reasonable Faith: Christian Truth and Apologetics,* Third Edition. Crossway, 2008. See Chapter 8: "The Resurrection of Jesus."
   - Wright, N.T. *Jesus and the Victory of God.* Fortress Press, 1996.
   - Wright, N.T. *The Resurrection of the Son of God.* Fortress Press, 2003.
   - Ehrman, Bart D. *Did Jesus Exist?: The Historical Argument for Jesus of Nazareth.* HarperOne, 2012.
     - o Note that even skeptics like Ehrman affirm the historical existence of Jesus.

2. Jesus's Claims to Deity
   - Blomberg, Craig L. *Jesus and the Gospels: An Introduction and Survey.* B&H Academic, 2009.
   - Lewis. *Mere Christianity.* See the famous "liar, lunatic, or lord" argument in Book II, Chapter 3: "The Shocking Alternative."
   - Bauckham, Richard. *Jesus and the God of Israel: God Crucified and Other Studies on the New Testament's Christology of Divine Identity.* William B. Eerdmans, 2008.

3. Early Christian Belief in the Resurrection
   - Habermas. *The Historical Jesus.*
   - Hurtado, Larry. *Lord Jesus Christ: Devotion to Jesus in Earliest Christianity.* William B. Eerdmans, 2003.
   - Craig, William Lane. *Assessing the New Testament Evidence for the Historicity of the Resurrection of Jesus.* Edwin Mellen Press, 1989.

4. The Minimal Facts Approach
   - Habermas, Gary R. "Minimal Facts on the Resurrection of Jesus: the Role of Methodology as a Crucial Component in Establishing Historicity." Liberty University School of Divinity, Scholars Crossing, Faculty Publications and Presentations 14 (2012). https://digitalcommons.liberty.edu/cgi/viewcontent.cgi?article=1014&context=sod_fac_pubs.
   - Habermas and Licona. *The Case for the Resurrection of Jesus.* There are multiple articles and lectures on the minimal facts cited and summarized in this book.
     - o Minimal facts include:
       - Jesus's death by crucifixion
       - Empty tomb
       - Post-resurrection appearances

- Early belief by disciples
- Conversion of Paul and James

5. Non-Christian Sources Mentioning Jesus
   - Josephus. *Antiquities* 18.3.3. This section is commonly referred to as *Testimonium Flavianum.*
   - Tacitus. *Annals* 15.44.
   - Pliny the Younger. *Letters* 10.96.
   - Suetonius. *The Lives of the Caesars.*

6. The Empty Tomb
   - Craig. *Reasonable Faith.* See Chapter 8: "The Resurrection of Jesus."
   - Wright. *The Resurrection of the Son of God.*

7. The Changed Lives of the Disciples
   - Blaiklock, E.M. *The Archaeology of the New Testament.* Zondervan, 1970.
   - Anderson, J.N.D. *Christianity: The Witness of History.* InterVarsity Press, 1970.

8. Alternative Theories
   - McDowell and McDowell. *Evidence That Demands a Verdict.*
   - Habermas and Licona. *The Case for the Resurrection of Jesus.*
   - Craig. *On Guard.*

ADDITIONAL SUGGESTED READING
- Wright, N.T. *Surprised by Hope: Rethinking Heaven, the Resurrection, and the Mission of the Church.* HarperOne, 2008.
- Keener, Craig S. *Miracles: The Credibility of the New Testament Accounts.* Baker Academic, 2011.

CHAPTER 10: THE NEXT STEP

1. The Nature of Saving Faith
   - Stott, John. *Basic Christianity*. InterVarsity Press, 2008. Originally published in 1958.
     - o Clear explanation of the Gospel and personal decision.
   - Packer, J.I. *Knowing God*. InterVarsity Press, 1973.
     - o Classic book on moving from head knowledge to a personal relationship.
   - Keller, Timothy. *The Reason for God: Belief in an Age of Skepticism*. Dutton, 2008.
     - o Includes helpful section on the difference between mere belief and personal trust.

2. Faith and Reason Working Together
   - Moreland, J.P. *Love Your God with All Your Mind: The Role of Reason in the Life of the Soul*. NavPress, 1997.
   - Craig. *On Guard*.

3. The Gospel Invitation
   - Romans 10:9 "If you declare with your mouth, 'Jesus is Lord,' and believe in your heart that God raised him from the dead, you will be saved."
   - Ephesians 2:8 "For it is by grace you have been saved, through faith . . ."
   - Revelation 3:20: "I stand at the door and knock . . ."

4. The Simplicity of Receiving Christ
   - Bright, Bill. *Have You Heard of the Four Spiritual Laws?* New Life Publications, 2016. Originally published in 1952.
   - McDowell, Josh and Sean McDowell. *More Than a Carpenter*. Tyndale, 2009.

5. Growing in Faith After the Decision
   - Stanley, Charles. *Handbook for Christian Living*. Thomas Nelson, 1996.
   - *The 2:7 Series: Growing Strong in God's Family*. NavPress, 1991.
     - o Classic basic discipleship material for new believers.

6. The Ongoing Invitation to Seek
   - Jeremiah 29:13 "You will seek me and find me when you seek me with all your heart."
   - John 1:12 "Yet to all who did receive him, to those who believed in his name, he gave the right to become children of God."

ADDITIONAL SUGGESTED READING

- Strobel, Lee. *The Case for Faith*. Zondervan, 2000.
- Guinness, Os. *Long Journey Home: A Guide to Your Search for the Meaning of Life*. WaterBrook, 2001.

GOSPEL OF JOHN |

1

¹ In the beginning was the Word, and the Word was with God, and the Word was God. ² The same was in the beginning with God. ³ All things were made through him. Without him, nothing was made that has been made. ⁴ In him was life, and the life was the light of men. ⁵ The light shines in the darkness, and the darkness hasn't overcome it.

⁶ There came a man sent from God, whose name was John. ⁷ The same came as a witness, that he might testify about the light, that all might believe through him. ⁸ He was not the light, but was sent that he might testify about the light. ⁹ The true light that enlightens everyone was coming into the world.

¹⁰ He was in the world, and the world was made through him, and the world didn't recognize him. ¹¹ He came to his own, and those who were his own didn't receive him. ¹² But as many as received him, to them he gave the right to become God's children, to those who believe in his name: ¹³ who were born, not of blood, nor of the will of the flesh, nor of the will of man, but of God.

¹⁴ The Word became flesh and lived among us. We saw his glory, such glory as of the only born Son of the Father, full of grace and truth. ¹⁵ John testified about him. He cried out, saying, "This

was he of whom I said, 'He who comes after me has surpassed me, for he was before me.' " [16] From his fullness we all received grace upon grace. [17] For the law was given through Moses. Grace and truth were realized through Jesus Christ. [18] No one has seen God at any time. The only born Son, who is in the bosom of the Father, has declared him.

[19] This is John's testimony, when the Jews sent priests and Levites from Jerusalem to ask him, "Who are you?"

[20] He declared, and didn't deny, but he declared, "I am not the Christ."

[21] They asked him, "What then? Are you Elijah?"

He said, "I am not."

"Are you the prophet?"

He answered, "No."

[22] They said therefore to him, "Who are you? Give us an answer to take back to those who sent us. What do you say about yourself?"

[23] He said, "I am the voice of one crying in the wilderness, 'Make straight the way of the Lord,' as Isaiah the prophet said."

[24] The ones who had been sent were from the Pharisees. [25] They asked him, "Why then do you baptize if you are not the Christ, nor Elijah, nor the prophet?"

[26] John answered them, "I baptize in water, but among you stands one whom you don't know. [27] He is the one who comes after me, who is preferred before me, whose sandal strap I'm not worthy to loosen." [28] These things were done in Bethany beyond the Jordan, where John was baptizing.

[29] The next day, he saw Jesus coming to him, and said, "Behold, the Lamb of God, who takes away the sin of the world! [30] This is he of whom I said, 'After me comes a man who is preferred before me, for he was before me.' [31] I didn't know him, but for this reason I came baptizing in water, that he would be revealed to Israel."

³² John testified, saying, "I have seen the Spirit descending like a dove out of heaven, and it remained on him. ³³ I didn't recognize him, but he who sent me to baptize in water said to me, 'On whomever you will see the Spirit descending and remaining on him is he who baptizes in the Holy Spirit.' ³⁴ I have seen and have testified that this is the Son of God."

³⁵ Again, the next day, John was standing with two of his disciples, ³⁶ and he looked at Jesus as he walked, and said, "Behold, the Lamb of God!" ³⁷ The two disciples heard him speak, and they followed Jesus. ³⁸ Jesus turned and saw them following, and said to them, "What are you looking for?"

They said to him, "Rabbi" (which is to say, being interpreted, Teacher), "where are you staying?"

³⁹ He said to them, "Come and see."

They came and saw where he was staying, and they stayed with him that day. It was about the tenth hour. ⁴⁰ One of the two who heard John and followed him was Andrew, Simon Peter's brother. ⁴¹ He first found his own brother, Simon, and said to him, "We have found the Messiah!" (which is, being interpreted, Christ). ⁴² He brought him to Jesus. Jesus looked at him and said, "You are Simon the son of Jonah. You shall be called Cephas" (which is by interpretation, Peter).

⁴³ On the next day, he was determined to go out into Galilee, and he found Philip. Jesus said to him, "Follow me." ⁴⁴ Now Philip was from Bethsaida, the city of Andrew and Peter. ⁴⁵ Philip found Nathanael, and said to him, "We have found him of whom Moses in the law and also the prophets, wrote: Jesus of Nazareth, the son of Joseph."

⁴⁶ Nathanael said to him, "Can any good thing come out of Nazareth?"

Philip said to him, "Come and see."

⁴⁷ Jesus saw Nathanael coming to him, and said about him, "Behold, an Israelite indeed, in whom is no deceit!"

⁴⁸ Nathanael said to him, "How do you know me?"

Jesus answered him, "Before Philip called you, when you were under the fig tree, I saw you."

⁴⁹ Nathanael answered him, "Rabbi, you are the Son of God! You are King of Israel!"

⁵⁰ Jesus answered him, "Because I told you, 'I saw you underneath the fig tree,' do you believe? You will see greater things than these!" ⁵¹ He said to him, "Most certainly, I tell you all, hereafter you will see heaven opened, and the angels of God ascending and descending on the Son of Man."

2̄

¹ The third day, there was a wedding in Cana of Galilee. Jesus' mother was there. ² Jesus also was invited, with his disciples, to the wedding. ³ When the wine ran out, Jesus' mother said to him, "They have no wine."

⁴ Jesus said to her, "Woman, what does that have to do with you and me? My hour has not yet come."

⁵ His mother said to the servants, "Whatever he says to you, do it."

⁶ Now there were six water pots of stone set there after the Jews' way of purifying, containing two or three metretes apiece. ⁷ Jesus said to them, "Fill the water pots with water." So they filled them up to the brim. ⁸ He said to them, "Now draw some out, and take it to the ruler of the feast." So they took it. ⁹ When the ruler of the feast tasted the water now become wine, and didn't know where it came from (but the servants who had drawn the water knew), the ruler of the feast called the bridegroom ¹⁰ and

said to him, "Everyone serves the good wine first, and when the guests have drunk freely, then that which is worse. You have kept the good wine until now!" ¹¹ This beginning of his signs Jesus did in Cana of Galilee, and revealed his glory; and his disciples believed in him.

¹² After this, he went down to Capernaum, he, and his mother, his brothers, and his disciples; and they stayed there a few days.

¹³ The Passover of the Jews was at hand, and Jesus went up to Jerusalem. ¹⁴ He found in the temple those who sold oxen, sheep, and doves, and the changers of money sitting. ¹⁵ He made a whip of cords and drove all out of the temple, both the sheep and the oxen; and he poured out the changers' money and overthrew their tables. ¹⁶ To those who sold the doves, he said, "Take these things out of here! Don't make my Father's house a marketplace!" ¹⁷ His disciples remembered that it was written, "Zeal for your house will eat me up."

¹⁸ The Jews therefore answered him, "What sign do you show us, seeing that you do these things?"

¹⁹ Jesus answered them, "Destroy this temple, and in three days I will raise it up."

²⁰ The Jews therefore said, "It took forty-six years to build this temple! Will you raise it up in three days?" ²¹ But he spoke of the temple of his body. ²² When therefore he was raised from the dead, his disciples remembered that he said this, and they believed the Scripture and the word which Jesus had said.

²³ Now when he was in Jerusalem at the Passover, during the feast, many believed in his name, observing his signs which he did. ²⁴ But Jesus didn't entrust himself to them, because he knew everyone, ²⁵ and because he didn't need for anyone to testify concerning man; for he himself knew what was in man.

3

¹ Now there was a man of the Pharisees named Nicodemus, a ruler of the Jews. ² He came to Jesus by night and said to him, "Rabbi, we know that you are a teacher come from God, for no one can do these signs that you do, unless God is with him."

³ Jesus answered him, "Most certainly I tell you, unless one is born anew, he can't see God's Kingdom."

⁴ Nicodemus said to him, "How can a man be born when he is old? Can he enter a second time into his mother's womb and be born?"

⁵ Jesus answered, "Most certainly I tell you, unless one is born of water and Spirit, he can't enter into God's Kingdom. ⁶ That which is born of the flesh is flesh. That which is born of the Spirit is spirit. ⁷ Don't marvel that I said to you, 'You must be born anew.' ⁸ The wind blows where it wants to, and you hear its sound, but don't know where it comes from and where it is going. So is everyone who is born of the Spirit."

⁹ Nicodemus answered him, "How can these things be?"

¹⁰ Jesus answered him, "Are you the teacher of Israel, and don't understand these things? ¹¹ Most certainly I tell you, we speak that which we know and testify of that which we have seen, and you don't receive our witness. ¹² If I told you earthly things and you don't believe, how will you believe if I tell you heavenly things? ¹³ No one has ascended into heaven but he who descended out of heaven, the Son of Man, who is in heaven. ¹⁴ As Moses lifted up the serpent in the wilderness, even so must the Son of Man be lifted up, ¹⁵ that whoever believes in him should not perish, but have eternal life. ¹⁶ For God so loved the world, that he gave his only born Son, that whoever believes in him should not perish, but have eternal life. ¹⁷ For God didn't send his Son into the world to judge the world, but that the world should be

saved through him. [18] He who believes in him is not judged. He who doesn't believe has been judged already, because he has not believed in the name of the only born Son of God. [19] This is the judgment, that the light has come into the world, and men loved the darkness rather than the light, for their works were evil. [20] For everyone who does evil hates the light and doesn't come to the light, lest his works would be exposed. [21] But he who does the truth comes to the light, that his works may be revealed, that they have been done in God."

[22] After these things, Jesus came with his disciples into the land of Judea. He stayed there with them and baptized. [23] John also was baptizing in Enon near Salim, because there was much water there. They came and were baptized; [24] for John was not yet thrown into prison. [25] Therefore a dispute arose on the part of John's disciples with some Jews about purification. [26] They came to John and said to him, "Rabbi, he who was with you beyond the Jordan, to whom you have testified, behold, he baptizes, and everyone is coming to him."

[27] John answered, "A man can receive nothing unless it has been given him from heaven. [28] You yourselves testify that I said, 'I am not the Christ,' but, 'I have been sent before him.' [29] He who has the bride is the bridegroom; but the friend of the bridegroom, who stands and hears him, rejoices greatly because of the bridegroom's voice. Therefore my joy is made full. [30] He must increase, but I must decrease.

[31] "He who comes from above is above all. He who is from the earth belongs to the earth and speaks of the earth. He who comes from heaven is above all. [32] What he has seen and heard, of that he testifies; and no one receives his witness. [33] He who has received his witness has set his seal to this, that God is true. [34] For he whom God has sent speaks the words of God; for God gives the Spirit without measure. [35] The Father loves the Son,

and has given all things into his hand. [36] One who believes in the Son has eternal life, but one who disobeys the Son won't see life, but the wrath of God remains on him."

4

[1] Therefore when the Lord knew that the Pharisees had heard that Jesus was making and baptizing more disciples than John [2] (although Jesus himself didn't baptize, but his disciples), [3] he left Judea and departed into Galilee. [4] He needed to pass through Samaria. [5] So he came to a city of Samaria called Sychar, near the parcel of ground that Jacob gave to his son Joseph. [6] Jacob's well was there. Jesus therefore, being tired from his journey, sat down by the well. It was about the sixth hour.

[7] A woman of Samaria came to draw water. Jesus said to her, "Give me a drink." [8] For his disciples had gone away into the city to buy food.

[9] The Samaritan woman therefore said to him, "How is it that you, being a Jew, ask for a drink from me, a Samaritan woman?" (For Jews have no dealings with Samaritans.)

[10] Jesus answered her, "If you knew the gift of God, and who it is who says to you, 'Give me a drink,' you would have asked him, and he would have given you living water."

[11] The woman said to him, "Sir, you have nothing to draw with, and the well is deep. So where do you get that living water? [12] Are you greater than our father Jacob, who gave us the well and drank from it himself, as did his children and his livestock?"

[13] Jesus answered her, "Everyone who drinks of this water will thirst again, [14] but whoever drinks of the water that I will give him will never thirst again; but the water that I will give him will become in him a well of water springing up to eternal life."

[15] The woman said to him, "Sir, give me this water, so that I don't get thirsty, neither come all the way here to draw."

[16] Jesus said to her, "Go, call your husband, and come here."

[17] The woman answered, "I have no husband."

Jesus said to her, "You said well, 'I have no husband,' [18] for you have had five husbands; and he whom you now have is not your husband. This you have said truly."

[19] The woman said to him, "Sir, I perceive that you are a prophet. [20] Our fathers worshiped in this mountain, and you Jews say that in Jerusalem is the place where people ought to worship."

[21] Jesus said to her, "Woman, believe me, the hour is coming when neither in this mountain nor in Jerusalem will you worship the Father. [22] You worship that which you don't know. We worship that which we know; for salvation is from the Jews. [23] But the hour comes, and now is, when the true worshipers will worship the Father in spirit and truth, for the Father seeks such to be his worshipers. [24] God is spirit, and those who worship him must worship in spirit and truth."

[25] The woman said to him, "I know that Messiah is coming, he who is called Christ. When he has come, he will declare to us all things."

[26] Jesus said to her, "I am he, the one who speaks to you."

[27] Just then, his disciples came. They marveled that he was speaking with a woman; yet no one said, "What are you looking for?" or, "Why do you speak with her?" [28] So the woman left her water pot, went away into the city, and said to the people, [29] "Come, see a man who told me everything that I have done. Can this be the Christ?" [30] They went out of the city, and were coming to him.

[31] In the meanwhile, the disciples urged him, saying, "Rabbi, eat."

[32] But he said to them, "I have food to eat that you don't know about."

[33] The disciples therefore said to one another, "Has anyone brought him something to eat?"

[34] Jesus said to them, "My food is to do the will of him who sent me and to accomplish his work. [35] Don't you say, 'There are yet four months until the harvest'? Behold, I tell you, lift up your eyes and look at the fields, that they are white for harvest already. [36] He who reaps receives wages and gathers fruit to eternal life, that both he who sows and he who reaps may rejoice together. [37] For in this the saying is true, 'One sows, and another reaps.' [38] I sent you to reap that for which you haven't labored. Others have labored, and you have entered into their labor."

[39] From that city many of the Samaritans believed in him because of the word of the woman, who testified, "He told me everything that I have done." [40] So when the Samaritans came to him, they begged him to stay with them. He stayed there two days. [41] Many more believed because of his word. [42] They said to the woman, "Now we believe, not because of your speaking; for we have heard for ourselves, and know that this is indeed the Christ, the Savior of the world."

[43] After the two days he went out from there and went into Galilee. [44] For Jesus himself testified that a prophet has no honor in his own country. [45] So when he came into Galilee, the Galileans received him, having seen all the things that he did in Jerusalem at the feast, for they also went to the feast. [46] Jesus came therefore again to Cana of Galilee, where he made the water into wine. There was a certain nobleman whose son was sick at Capernaum. [47] When he heard that Jesus had come out of Judea into Galilee, he went to him and begged him that he would come down and heal his son, for he was at the point of death. [48] Jesus therefore said to him, "Unless you see signs and wonders, you will in no way believe."

⁴⁹ The nobleman said to him, "Sir, come down before my child dies."

⁵⁰ Jesus said to him, "Go your way. Your son lives." The man believed the word that Jesus spoke to him, and he went his way. ⁵¹ As he was going down, his servants met him and reported, saying "Your child lives!" ⁵² So he inquired of them the hour when he began to get better. They said therefore to him, "Yesterday at the seventh hour, the fever left him." ⁵³ So the father knew that it was at that hour in which Jesus said to him, "Your son lives." He believed, as did his whole house. ⁵⁴ This is again the second sign that Jesus did, having come out of Judea into Galilee.

5

¹ After these things, there was a feast of the Jews, and Jesus went up to Jerusalem. ² Now in Jerusalem by the sheep gate, there is a pool, which is called in Hebrew, "Bethesda", having five porches. ³ In these lay a great multitude of those who were sick, blind, lame, or paralyzed, waiting for the moving of the water; ⁴ for an angel went down at certain times into the pool and stirred up the water. Whoever stepped in first after the stirring of the water was healed of whatever disease he had. ⁵ A certain man was there who had been sick for thirty-eight years. ⁶ When Jesus saw him lying there, and knew that he had been sick for a long time, he asked him, "Do you want to be made well?"

⁷ The sick man answered him, "Sir, I have no one to put me into the pool when the water is stirred up, but while I'm coming, another steps down before me."

⁸ Jesus said to him, "Arise, take up your mat, and walk."

⁹ Immediately, the man was made well, and took up his mat and walked.

Now that day was a Sabbath. ¹⁰ So the Jews said to him who was cured, "It is the Sabbath. It is not lawful for you to carry the mat."

¹¹ He answered them, "He who made me well said to me, 'Take up your mat and walk.'"

¹² Then they asked him, "Who is the man who said to you, 'Take up your mat and walk'?"

¹³ But he who was healed didn't know who it was, for Jesus had withdrawn, a crowd being in the place.

¹⁴ Afterward Jesus found him in the temple and said to him, "Behold, you are made well. Sin no more, so that nothing worse happens to you."

¹⁵ The man went away, and told the Jews that it was Jesus who had made him well. ¹⁶ For this cause the Jews persecuted Jesus and sought to kill him, because he did these things on the Sabbath. ¹⁷ But Jesus answered them, "My Father is still working, so I am working, too."

¹⁸ For this cause therefore the Jews sought all the more to kill him, because he not only broke the Sabbath, but also called God his own Father, making himself equal with God. ¹⁹ Jesus therefore answered them, "Most certainly, I tell you, the Son can do nothing of himself, but what he sees the Father doing. For whatever things he does, these the Son also does likewise. ²⁰ For the Father has affection for the Son, and shows him all things that he himself does. He will show him greater works than these, that you may marvel. ²¹ For as the Father raises the dead and gives them life, even so the Son also gives life to whom he desires. ²² For the Father judges no one, but he has given all judgment to the Son, ²³ that all may honor the Son, even as they honor the Father. He who doesn't honor the Son doesn't honor the Father who sent him.

²⁴ "Most certainly I tell you, he who hears my word and believes him who sent me has eternal life, and doesn't come into judgment, but has passed out of death into life. ²⁵ Most certainly I tell you, the hour comes, and now is, when the dead will hear the Son of God's voice; and those who hear will live. ²⁶ For as the Father has life in himself, even so he gave to the Son also to have life in himself. ²⁷ He also gave him authority to execute judgment, because he is a son of man. ²⁸ Don't marvel at this, for the hour comes in which all who are in the tombs will hear his voice ²⁹ and will come out; those who have done good, to the resurrection of life; and those who have done evil, to the resurrection of judgment. ³⁰ I can of myself do nothing. As I hear, I judge; and my judgment is righteous, because I don't seek my own will, but the will of my Father who sent me.

³¹ "If I testify about myself, my witness is not valid. ³² It is another who testifies about me. I know that the testimony which he testifies about me is true. ³³ You have sent to John, and he has testified to the truth. ³⁴ But the testimony which I receive is not from man. However, I say these things that you may be saved. ³⁵ He was the burning and shining lamp, and you were willing to rejoice for a while in his light. ³⁶ But the testimony which I have is greater than that of John; for the works which the Father gave me to accomplish, the very works that I do, testify about me, that the Father has sent me. ³⁷ The Father himself, who sent me, has testified about me. You have neither heard his voice at any time, nor seen his form. ³⁸ You don't have his word living in you, because you don't believe him whom he sent.

³⁹ "You search the Scriptures, because you think that in them you have eternal life; and these are they which testify about me. ⁴⁰ Yet you will not come to me, that you may have life. ⁴¹ I don't receive glory from men. ⁴² But I know you, that you don't have God's love in yourselves. ⁴³ I have come in my Father's name,

and you don't receive me. If another comes in his own name, you will receive him. ⁴⁴ How can you believe, who receive glory from one another, and you don't seek the glory that comes from the only God?

⁴⁵ "Don't think that I will accuse you to the Father. There is one who accuses you, even Moses, on whom you have set your hope. ⁴⁶ For if you believed Moses, you would believe me; for he wrote about me. ⁴⁷ But if you don't believe his writings, how will you believe my words?"

6

¹ After these things, Jesus went away to the other side of the sea of Galilee, which is also called the Sea of Tiberias. ² A great multitude followed him, because they saw his signs which he did on those who were sick. ³ Jesus went up into the mountain, and he sat there with his disciples. ⁴ Now the Passover, the feast of the Jews, was at hand. ⁵ Jesus therefore, lifting up his eyes and seeing that a great multitude was coming to him, said to Philip, "Where are we to buy bread, that these may eat?" ⁶ He said this to test him, for he himself knew what he would do.

⁷ Philip answered him, "Two hundred denarii worth of bread is not sufficient for them, that every one of them may receive a little."

⁸ One of his disciples, Andrew, Simon Peter's brother, said to him, ⁹ "There is a boy here who has five barley loaves and two fish, but what are these among so many?"

¹⁰ Jesus said, "Have the people sit down." Now there was much grass in that place. So the men sat down, in number about five thousand. ¹¹ Jesus took the loaves, and having given thanks, he distributed to the disciples, and the disciples to those who were

sitting down, likewise also of the fish as much as they desired. [12] When they were filled, he said to his disciples, "Gather up the broken pieces which are left over, that nothing be lost." [13] So they gathered them up, and filled twelve baskets with broken pieces from the five barley loaves, which were left over by those who had eaten. [14] When therefore the people saw the sign which Jesus did, they said, "This is truly the prophet who comes into the world." [15] Jesus therefore, perceiving that they were about to come and take him by force to make him king, withdrew again to the mountain by himself.

[16] When evening came, his disciples went down to the sea. [17] They entered into the boat, and were going over the sea to Capernaum. It was now dark, and Jesus had not come to them. [18] The sea was tossed by a great wind blowing. [19] When therefore they had rowed about twenty-five or thirty stadia, they saw Jesus walking on the sea and drawing near to the boat; and they were afraid. [20] But he said to them, "It is I. Don't be afraid." [21] They were willing therefore to receive him into the boat. Immediately the boat was at the land where they were going.

[22] On the next day, the multitude that stood on the other side of the sea saw that there was no other boat there, except the one in which his disciples had embarked, and that Jesus hadn't entered with his disciples into the boat, but his disciples had gone away alone. [23] However, boats from Tiberias came near to the place where they ate the bread after the Lord had given thanks. [24] When the multitude therefore saw that Jesus wasn't there, nor his disciples, they themselves got into the boats and came to Capernaum, seeking Jesus. [25] When they found him on the other side of the sea, they asked him, "Rabbi, when did you come here?"

[26] Jesus answered them, "Most certainly I tell you, you seek me, not because you saw signs, but because you ate of the loaves

and were filled. ²⁷ Don't work for the food which perishes, but for the food which remains to eternal life, which the Son of Man will give to you. For God the Father has sealed him."

²⁸ They said therefore to him, "What must we do, that we may work the works of God?"

²⁹ Jesus answered them, "This is the work of God, that you believe in him whom he has sent."

³⁰ They said therefore to him, "What then do you do for a sign, that we may see and believe you? What work do you do? ³¹ Our fathers ate the manna in the wilderness. As it is written, 'He gave them bread out of heaven to eat.' "

³² Jesus therefore said to them, "Most certainly, I tell you, it wasn't Moses who gave you the bread out of heaven, but my Father gives you the true bread out of heaven. ³³ For the bread of God is that which comes down out of heaven and gives life to the world."

³⁴ They said therefore to him, "Lord, always give us this bread."

³⁵ Jesus said to them, "I am the bread of life. Whoever comes to me will not be hungry, and whoever believes in me will never be thirsty. ³⁶ But I told you that you have seen me, and yet you don't believe. ³⁷ All those whom the Father gives me will come to me. He who comes to me I will in no way throw out. ³⁸ For I have come down from heaven, not to do my own will, but the will of him who sent me. ³⁹ This is the will of my Father who sent me, that of all he has given to me I should lose nothing, but should raise him up at the last day. ⁴⁰ This is the will of the one who sent me, that everyone who sees the Son and believes in him should have eternal life; and I will raise him up at the last day."

⁴¹ The Jews therefore murmured concerning him, because he said, "I am the bread which came down out of heaven." ⁴² They said, "Isn't this Jesus, the son of Joseph, whose father and mother we know? How then does he say, 'I have come down out of heaven'?"

⁴³ Therefore Jesus answered them, "Don't murmur among yourselves. ⁴⁴ No one can come to me unless the Father who sent me draws him; and I will raise him up in the last day. ⁴⁵ It is written in the prophets, 'They will all be taught by God.' Therefore everyone who hears from the Father and has learned, comes to me. ⁴⁶ Not that anyone has seen the Father, except he who is from God. He has seen the Father. ⁴⁷ Most certainly, I tell you, he who believes in me has eternal life. ⁴⁸ I am the bread of life. ⁴⁹ Your fathers ate the manna in the wilderness and they died. ⁵⁰ This is the bread which comes down out of heaven, that anyone may eat of it and not die. ⁵¹ I am the living bread which came down out of heaven. If anyone eats of this bread, he will live forever. Yes, the bread which I will give for the life of the world is my flesh."

⁵² The Jews therefore contended with one another, saying, "How can this man give us his flesh to eat?"

⁵³ Jesus therefore said to them, "Most certainly I tell you, unless you eat the flesh of the Son of Man and drink his blood, you don't have life in yourselves. ⁵⁴ He who eats my flesh and drinks my blood has eternal life, and I will raise him up at the last day. ⁵⁵ For my flesh is food indeed, and my blood is drink indeed. ⁵⁶ He who eats my flesh and drinks my blood lives in me, and I in him. ⁵⁷ As the living Father sent me, and I live because of the Father, so he who feeds on me will also live because of me. ⁵⁸ This is the bread which came down out of heaven—not as our fathers ate the manna and died. He who eats this bread will live forever." ⁵⁹ He said these things in the synagogue, as he taught in Capernaum.

⁶⁰ Therefore many of his disciples, when they heard this, said, "This is a hard saying! Who can listen to it?"

⁶¹ But Jesus knowing in himself that his disciples murmured at this, said to them, "Does this cause you to stumble? ⁶² Then

what if you would see the Son of Man ascending to where he was before? [63] It is the spirit who gives life. The flesh profits nothing. The words that I speak to you are spirit, and are life. [64] But there are some of you who don't believe." For Jesus knew from the beginning who they were who didn't believe, and who it was who would betray him. [65] He said, "For this cause I have said to you that no one can come to me, unless it is given to him by my Father."

[66] At this, many of his disciples went back and walked no more with him. [67] Jesus said therefore to the twelve, "You don't also want to go away, do you?"

[68] Simon Peter answered him, "Lord, to whom would we go? You have the words of eternal life. [69] We have come to believe and know that you are the Christ, the Son of the living God."

[70] Jesus answered them, "Didn't I choose you, the twelve, and one of you is a devil?" [71] Now he spoke of Judas, the son of Simon Iscariot, for it was he who would betray him, being one of the twelve.

7

[1] After these things, Jesus was walking in Galilee, for he wouldn't walk in Judea, because the Jews sought to kill him. [2] Now the feast of the Jews, the Feast of Booths, was at hand. [3] His brothers therefore said to him, "Depart from here and go into Judea, that your disciples also may see your works which you do. [4] For no one does anything in secret while he seeks to be known openly. If you do these things, reveal yourself to the world." [5] For even his brothers didn't believe in him.

[6] Jesus therefore said to them, "My time has not yet come, but your time is always ready. [7] The world can't hate you, but it

hates me, because I testify about it, that its works are evil. ⁸ You go up to the feast. I am not yet going up to this feast, because my time is not yet fulfilled."

⁹ Having said these things to them, he stayed in Galilee. ¹⁰ But when his brothers had gone up to the feast, then he also went up, not publicly, but as it were in secret. ¹¹ The Jews therefore sought him at the feast, and said, "Where is he?" ¹² There was much murmuring among the multitudes concerning him. Some said, "He is a good man." Others said, "Not so, but he leads the multitude astray." ¹³ Yet no one spoke openly of him for fear of the Jews. ¹⁴ But when it was now the middle of the feast, Jesus went up into the temple and taught. ¹⁵ The Jews therefore marveled, saying, "How does this man know letters, having never been educated?"

¹⁶ Jesus therefore answered them, "My teaching is not mine, but his who sent me. ¹⁷ If anyone desires to do his will, he will know about the teaching, whether it is from God or if I am speaking from myself. ¹⁸ He who speaks from himself seeks his own glory, but he who seeks the glory of him who sent him is true, and no unrighteousness is in him. ¹⁹ Didn't Moses give you the law, and yet none of you keeps the law? Why do you seek to kill me?"

²⁰ The multitude answered, "You have a demon! Who seeks to kill you?"

²¹ Jesus answered them, "I did one work and you all marvel because of it. ²² Moses has given you circumcision (not that it is of Moses, but of the fathers), and on the Sabbath you circumcise a boy. ²³ If a boy receives circumcision on the Sabbath, that the law of Moses may not be broken, are you angry with me because I made a man completely healthy on the Sabbath? ²⁴ Don't judge according to appearance, but judge righteous judgment."

²⁵ Therefore some of them of Jerusalem said, "Isn't this he whom they seek to kill? ²⁶ Behold, he speaks openly, and they say

nothing to him. Can it be that the rulers indeed know that this is truly the Christ? [27] However, we know where this man comes from, but when the Christ comes, no one will know where he comes from."

[28] Jesus therefore cried out in the temple, teaching and saying, "You both know me, and know where I am from. I have not come of myself, but he who sent me is true, whom you don't know. [29] I know him, because I am from him, and he sent me."

[30] They sought therefore to take him; but no one laid a hand on him, because his hour had not yet come. [31] But of the multitude, many believed in him. They said, "When the Christ comes, he won't do more signs than those which this man has done, will he?" [32] The Pharisees heard the multitude murmuring these things concerning him, and the chief priests and the Pharisees sent officers to arrest him.

[33] Then Jesus said, "I will be with you a little while longer, then I go to him who sent me. [34] You will seek me and won't find me. You can't come where I am."

[35] The Jews therefore said among themselves, "Where will this man go that we won't find him? Will he go to the Dispersion among the Greeks and teach the Greeks? [36] What is this word that he said, 'You will seek me, and won't find me;' and 'Where I am, you can't come'?"

[37] Now on the last and greatest day of the feast, Jesus stood and cried out, "If anyone is thirsty, let him come to me and drink! [38] He who believes in me, as the Scripture has said, from within him will flow rivers of living water." [39] But he said this about the Spirit, which those believing in him were to receive. For the Holy Spirit was not yet given, because Jesus wasn't yet glorified.

[40] Many of the multitude therefore, when they heard these words, said, "This is truly the prophet." [41] Others said, "This is the Christ." But some said, "What, does the Christ come out of

Galilee? ⁴²Hasn't the Scripture said that the Christ comes of the offspring of David, and from Bethlehem, the village where David was?" ⁴³So a division arose in the multitude because of him. ⁴⁴Some of them would have arrested him, but no one laid hands on him. ⁴⁵The officers therefore came to the chief priests and Pharisees; and they said to them, "Why didn't you bring him?"

⁴⁶The officers answered, "No man ever spoke like this man!"

⁴⁷The Pharisees therefore answered them, "You aren't also led astray, are you? ⁴⁸Have any of the rulers or any of the Pharisees believed in him? ⁴⁹But this multitude that doesn't know the law is cursed."

⁵⁰Nicodemus (he who came to him by night, being one of them) said to them, ⁵¹"Does our law judge a man unless it first hears from him personally and knows what he does?"

⁵²They answered him, "Are you also from Galilee? Search and see that no prophet has arisen out of Galilee."

⁵³Everyone went to his own house,

8

¹but Jesus went to the Mount of Olives.

²Now very early in the morning, he came again into the temple, and all the people came to him. He sat down and taught them. ³The scribes and the Pharisees brought a woman taken in adultery. Having set her in the middle, ⁴they told him, "Teacher, we found this woman in adultery, in the very act. ⁵Now in our law, Moses commanded us to stone such women. What then do you say about her?" ⁶They said this testing him, that they might have something to accuse him of.

But Jesus stooped down and wrote on the ground with his finger. ⁷But when they continued asking him, he looked up and said to them, "He who is without sin among you, let him throw the first stone at her." ⁸ Again he stooped down and wrote on the ground with his finger.

⁹ They, when they heard it, being convicted by their conscience, went out one by one, beginning from the oldest, even to the last. Jesus was left alone with the woman where she was, in the middle. ¹⁰ Jesus, standing up, saw her and said, "Woman, where are your accusers? Did no one condemn you?"

¹¹ She said, "No one, Lord."

Jesus said, "Neither do I condemn you. Go your way. From now on, sin no more."

¹² Again, therefore, Jesus spoke to them, saying, "I am the light of the world. He who follows me will not walk in the darkness, but will have the light of life."

¹³ The Pharisees therefore said to him, "You testify about yourself. Your testimony is not valid."

¹⁴ Jesus answered them, "Even if I testify about myself, my testimony is true, for I know where I came from, and where I am going; but you don't know where I came from, or where I am going. ¹⁵ You judge according to the flesh. I judge no one. ¹⁶ Even if I do judge, my judgment is true, for I am not alone, but I am with the Father who sent me. ¹⁷ It's also written in your law that the testimony of two people is valid. ¹⁸ I am one who testifies about myself, and the Father who sent me testifies about me."

¹⁹ They said therefore to him, "Where is your Father?"

Jesus answered, "You know neither me nor my Father. If you knew me, you would know my Father also." ²⁰ Jesus spoke these words in the treasury, as he taught in the temple. Yet no one arrested him, because his hour had not yet come. ²¹ Jesus said therefore again to them, "I am going away, and you will seek me, and you will die in your sins. Where I go, you can't come."

²² The Jews therefore said, "Will he kill himself, because he says, 'Where I am going, you can't come'?"

²³ He said to them, "You are from beneath. I am from above. You are of this world. I am not of this world. ²⁴ I said therefore to you that you will die in your sins; for unless you believe that I am he, you will die in your sins."

²⁵ They said therefore to him, "Who are you?"

Jesus said to them, "Just what I have been saying to you from the beginning. ²⁶ I have many things to speak and to judge concerning you. However, he who sent me is true; and the things which I heard from him, these I say to the world."

²⁷ They didn't understand that he spoke to them about the Father. ²⁸ Jesus therefore said to them, "When you have lifted up the Son of Man, then you will know that I am he, and I do nothing of myself, but as my Father taught me, I say these things. ²⁹ He who sent me is with me. The Father hasn't left me alone, for I always do the things that are pleasing to him."

³⁰ As he spoke these things, many believed in him. ³¹ Jesus therefore said to those Jews who had believed him, "If you remain in my word, then you are truly my disciples. ³² You will know the truth, and the truth will make you free."

³³ They answered him, "We are Abraham's offspring, and have never been in bondage to anyone. How do you say, 'You will be made free'?"

³⁴ Jesus answered them, "Most certainly I tell you, everyone who commits sin is the bondservant of sin. ³⁵ A bondservant doesn't live in the house forever. A son remains forever. ³⁶ If therefore the Son makes you free, you will be free indeed. ³⁷ I know that you are Abraham's offspring, yet you seek to kill me, because my word finds no place in you. ³⁸ I say the things which I have seen with my Father; and you also do the things which you have seen with your father."

[39] They answered him, "Our father is Abraham."

Jesus said to them, "If you were Abraham's children, you would do the works of Abraham. [40] But now you seek to kill me, a man who has told you the truth which I heard from God. Abraham didn't do this. [41] You do the works of your father."

They said to him, "We were not born of sexual immorality. We have one Father, God."

[42] Therefore Jesus said to them, "If God were your father, you would love me, for I came out and have come from God. For I haven't come of myself, but he sent me. [43] Why don't you understand my speech? Because you can't hear my word. [44] You are of your father the devil, and you want to do the desires of your father. He was a murderer from the beginning, and doesn't stand in the truth, because there is no truth in him. When he speaks a lie, he speaks on his own; for he is a liar, and the father of lies. [45] But because I tell the truth, you don't believe me. [46] Which of you convicts me of sin? If I tell the truth, why do you not believe me? [47] He who is of God hears the words of God. For this cause you don't hear, because you are not of God."

[48] Then the Jews answered him, "Don't we say well that you are a Samaritan, and have a demon?"

[49] Jesus answered, "I don't have a demon, but I honor my Father and you dishonor me. [50] But I don't seek my own glory. There is one who seeks and judges. [51] Most certainly, I tell you, if a person keeps my word, he will never see death."

[52] Then the Jews said to him, "Now we know that you have a demon. Abraham died, as did the prophets; and you say, 'If a man keeps my word, he will never taste of death.' [53] Are you greater than our father Abraham, who died? The prophets died. Who do you make yourself out to be?"

[54] Jesus answered, "If I glorify myself, my glory is nothing. It is my Father who glorifies me, of whom you say that he is our

God. [55] You have not known him, but I know him. If I said, 'I don't know him,' I would be like you, a liar. But I know him and keep his word. [56] Your father Abraham rejoiced to see my day. He saw it and was glad."

[57] The Jews therefore said to him, "You are not yet fifty years old! Have you seen Abraham?"

[58] Jesus said to them, "Most certainly, I tell you, before Abraham came into existence, I AM."

[59] Therefore they took up stones to throw at him, but Jesus hid himself and went out of the temple, having gone through the middle of them, and so passed by.

9

[1] As he passed by, he saw a man blind from birth. [2] His disciples asked him, "Rabbi, who sinned, this man or his parents, that he was born blind?"

[3] Jesus answered, "This man didn't sin, nor did his parents, but that the works of God might be revealed in him. [4] I must work the works of him who sent me while it is day. The night is coming, when no one can work. [5] While I am in the world, I am the light of the world." [6] When he had said this, he spat on the ground, made mud with the saliva, anointed the blind man's eyes with the mud, [7] and said to him, "Go, wash in the pool of Siloam" (which means "Sent"). So he went away, washed, and came back seeing.

[8] Therefore the neighbors and those who saw that he was blind before said, "Isn't this he who sat and begged?" [9] Others were saying, "It is he." Still others were saying, "He looks like him."

He said, "I am he."

[10] They therefore were asking him, "How were your eyes opened?"

[11] He answered, "A man called Jesus made mud, anointed my eyes, and said to me, 'Go to the pool of Siloam and wash.' So I went away and washed, and I received sight."

[12] Then they asked him, "Where is he?"

He said, "I don't know."

[13] They brought him who had been blind to the Pharisees. [14] It was a Sabbath when Jesus made the mud and opened his eyes. [15] Again therefore the Pharisees also asked him how he received his sight. He said to them, "He put mud on my eyes, I washed, and I see."

[16] Some therefore of the Pharisees said, "This man is not from God, because he doesn't keep the Sabbath."

Others said, "How can a man who is a sinner do such signs?" So there was division among them.

[17] Therefore they asked the blind man again, "What do you say about him, because he opened your eyes?"

He said, "He is a prophet."

[18] The Jews therefore didn't believe concerning him, that he had been blind and had received his sight, until they called the parents of him who had received his sight, [19] and asked them, "Is this your son, whom you say was born blind? How then does he now see?"

[20] His parents answered them, "We know that this is our son, and that he was born blind; [21] but how he now sees, we don't know; or who opened his eyes, we don't know. He is of age. Ask him. He will speak for himself." [22] His parents said these things because they feared the Jews; for the Jews had already agreed that if any man would confess him as Christ, he would be put out of the synagogue. [23] Therefore his parents said, "He is of age. Ask him."

[24] So they called the man who was blind a second time, and said to him, "Give glory to God. We know that this man is a sinner."

²⁵ He therefore answered, "I don't know if he is a sinner. One thing I do know: that though I was blind, now I see."

²⁶ They said to him again, "What did he do to you? How did he open your eyes?"

²⁷ He answered them, "I told you already, and you didn't listen. Why do you want to hear it again? You don't also want to become his disciples, do you?"

²⁸ They insulted him and said, "You are his disciple, but we are disciples of Moses. ²⁹ We know that God has spoken to Moses. But as for this man, we don't know where he comes from."

³⁰ The man answered them, "How amazing! You don't know where he comes from, yet he opened my eyes. ³¹ We know that God doesn't listen to sinners, but if anyone is a worshiper of God and does his will, he listens to him. ³² Since the world began it has never been heard of that anyone opened the eyes of someone born blind. ³³ If this man were not from God, he could do nothing."

³⁴ They answered him, "You were altogether born in sins, and do you teach us?" Then they threw him out.

³⁵ Jesus heard that they had thrown him out, and finding him, he said, "Do you believe in the Son of God?"

³⁶ He answered, "Who is he, Lord, that I may believe in him?"

³⁷ Jesus said to him, "You have both seen him, and it is he who speaks with you."

³⁸ He said, "Lord, I believe!" and he worshiped him.

³⁹ Jesus said, "I came into this world for judgment, that those who don't see may see; and that those who see may become blind."

⁴⁰ Those of the Pharisees who were with him heard these things, and said to him, "Are we also blind?"

⁴¹ Jesus said to them, "If you were blind, you would have no sin; but now you say, 'We see.' Therefore your sin remains.

10

¹ "Most certainly, I tell you, one who doesn't enter by the door into the sheep fold, but climbs up some other way, is a thief and a robber. ² But one who enters in by the door is the shepherd of the sheep. ³ The gatekeeper opens the gate for him, and the sheep listen to his voice. He calls his own sheep by name and leads them out. ⁴ Whenever he brings out his own sheep, he goes before them; and the sheep follow him, for they know his voice. ⁵ They will by no means follow a stranger, but will flee from him; for they don't know the voice of strangers." ⁶ Jesus spoke this parable to them, but they didn't understand what he was telling them.

⁷ Jesus therefore said to them again, "Most certainly, I tell you, I am the sheep's door. ⁸ All who came before me are thieves and robbers, but the sheep didn't listen to them. ⁹ I am the door. If anyone enters in by me, he will be saved, and will go in and go out and will find pasture. ¹⁰ The thief only comes to steal, kill, and destroy. I came that they may have life, and may have it abundantly.

¹¹ "I am the good shepherd. The good shepherd lays down his life for the sheep. ¹² He who is a hired hand, and not a shepherd, who doesn't own the sheep, sees the wolf coming, leaves the sheep, and flees. The wolf snatches the sheep and scatters them. ¹³ The hired hand flees because he is a hired hand and doesn't care for the sheep. ¹⁴ I am the good shepherd. I know my own, and I'm known by my own; ¹⁵ even as the Father knows me, and I know the Father. I lay down my life for the sheep. ¹⁶ I have other sheep which are not of this fold. I must bring them also, and they will hear my voice. They will become one flock with one shepherd. ¹⁷ Therefore the Father loves me, because I lay down my life, that I may take it again. ¹⁸ No one takes it away from me, but I lay it down by myself. I have power to lay it down,

and I have power to take it again. I received this commandment from my Father."

¹⁹ Therefore a division arose again among the Jews because of these words. ²⁰ Many of them said, "He has a demon and is insane! Why do you listen to him?" ²¹ Others said, "These are not the sayings of one possessed by a demon. It isn't possible for a demon to open the eyes of the blind, is it?"

²² It was the Feast of the Dedication at Jerusalem. ²³ It was winter, and Jesus was walking in the temple, in Solomon's porch. ²⁴ The Jews therefore came around him and said to him, "How long will you hold us in suspense? If you are the Christ, tell us plainly."

²⁵ Jesus answered them, "I told you, and you don't believe. The works that I do in my Father's name, these testify about me. ²⁶ But you don't believe, because you are not of my sheep, as I told you. ²⁷ My sheep hear my voice, and I know them, and they follow me. ²⁸ I give eternal life to them. They will never perish, and no one will snatch them out of my hand. ²⁹ My Father who has given them to me is greater than all. No one is able to snatch them out of my Father's hand. ³⁰ I and the Father are one."

³¹ Therefore the Jews took up stones again to stone him. ³² Jesus answered them, "I have shown you many good works from my Father. For which of those works do you stone me?"

³³ The Jews answered him, "We don't stone you for a good work, but for blasphemy, because you, being a man, make yourself God."

³⁴ Jesus answered them, "Isn't it written in your law, 'I said, you are gods'? ³⁵ If he called them gods, to whom the word of God came (and the Scripture can't be broken), ³⁶ do you say of him whom the Father sanctified and sent into the world, 'You blaspheme,' because I said, 'I am the Son of God'? ³⁷ If I don't do the works of my Father, don't believe me. ³⁸ But if I do them,

though you don't believe me, believe the works, that you may know and believe that the Father is in me, and I in the Father." [39] They sought again to seize him, and he went out of their hand. [40] He went away again beyond the Jordan into the place where John was baptizing at first, and he stayed there. [41] Many came to him. They said, "John indeed did no sign, but everything that John said about this man is true." [42] Many believed in him there.

11

[1] Now a certain man was sick, Lazarus from Bethany, of the village of Mary and her sister, Martha. [2] It was that Mary who had anointed the Lord with ointment and wiped his feet with her hair, whose brother Lazarus was sick. [3] The sisters therefore sent to him, saying, "Lord, behold, he for whom you have great affection is sick."

[4] But when Jesus heard it, he said, "This sickness is not to death, but for the glory of God, that God's Son may be glorified by it." [5] Now Jesus loved Martha, and her sister, and Lazarus. [6] When therefore he heard that he was sick, he stayed two days in the place where he was. [7] Then after this he said to the disciples, "Let's go into Judea again."

[8] The disciples asked him, "Rabbi, the Jews were just trying to stone you. Are you going there again?"

[9] Jesus answered, "Aren't there twelve hours of daylight? If a man walks in the day, he doesn't stumble, because he sees the light of this world. [10] But if a man walks in the night, he stumbles, because the light isn't in him." [11] He said these things, and after that, he said to them, "Our friend Lazarus has fallen asleep, but I am going so that I may awake him out of sleep."

[12] The disciples therefore said, "Lord, if he has fallen asleep, he will recover."

¹³ Now Jesus had spoken of his death, but they thought that he spoke of taking rest in sleep. ¹⁴ So Jesus said to them plainly then, "Lazarus is dead. ¹⁵ I am glad for your sakes that I was not there, so that you may believe. Nevertheless, let's go to him."

¹⁶ Thomas therefore, who is called Didymus, said to his fellow disciples, "Let's also go, that we may die with him."

¹⁷ So when Jesus came, he found that he had been in the tomb four days already. ¹⁸ Now Bethany was near Jerusalem, about fifteen stadia away. ¹⁹ Many of the Jews had joined the women around Martha and Mary, to console them concerning their brother. ²⁰ Then when Martha heard that Jesus was coming, she went and met him, but Mary stayed in the house. ²¹ Therefore Martha said to Jesus, "Lord, if you would have been here, my brother wouldn't have died. ²² Even now I know that whatever you ask of God, God will give you."

²³ Jesus said to her, "Your brother will rise again."

²⁴ Martha said to him, "I know that he will rise again in the resurrection at the last day."

²⁵ Jesus said to her, "I am the resurrection and the life. He who believes in me will still live, even if he dies. ²⁶ Whoever lives and believes in me will never die. Do you believe this?"

²⁷ She said to him, "Yes, Lord. I have come to believe that you are the Christ, God's Son, he who comes into the world."

²⁸ When she had said this, she went away and called Mary, her sister, secretly, saying, "The Teacher is here and is calling you."

²⁹ When she heard this, she arose quickly and went to him. ³⁰ Now Jesus had not yet come into the village, but was in the place where Martha met him. ³¹ Then the Jews who were with her in the house and were consoling her, when they saw Mary, that she rose up quickly and went out, followed her, saying, "She is going to the tomb to weep there."

[32] Therefore when Mary came to where Jesus was and saw him, she fell down at his feet, saying to him, "Lord, if you would have been here, my brother wouldn't have died."

[33] When Jesus therefore saw her weeping, and the Jews weeping who came with her, he groaned in the spirit and was troubled, [34] and said, "Where have you laid him?"

They told him, "Lord, come and see."

[35] Jesus wept.

[36] The Jews therefore said, "See how much affection he had for him!" [37] Some of them said, "Couldn't this man, who opened the eyes of him who was blind, have also kept this man from dying?"

[38] Jesus therefore, again groaning in himself, came to the tomb. Now it was a cave, and a stone lay against it. [39] Jesus said, "Take away the stone."

Martha, the sister of him who was dead, said to him, "Lord, by this time there is a stench, for he has been dead four days."

[40] Jesus said to her, "Didn't I tell you that if you believed, you would see God's glory?"

[41] So they took away the stone from the place where the dead man was lying. Jesus lifted up his eyes and said, "Father, I thank you that you listened to me. [42] I know that you always listen to me, but because of the multitude standing around I said this, that they may believe that you sent me." [43] When he had said this, he cried with a loud voice, "Lazarus, come out!"

[44] He who was dead came out, bound hand and foot with wrappings, and his face was wrapped around with a cloth.

Jesus said to them, "Free him, and let him go."

[45] Therefore many of the Jews who came to Mary and saw what Jesus did believed in him. [46] But some of them went away to the Pharisees and told them the things which Jesus had done. [47] The chief priests therefore and the Pharisees gathered a council, and said, "What are we doing? For this man does many signs. [48] If we

leave him alone like this, everyone will believe in him, and the Romans will come and take away both our place and our nation."

⁴⁹ But a certain one of them, Caiaphas, being high priest that year, said to them, "You know nothing at all, ⁵⁰ nor do you consider that it is advantageous for us that one man should die for the people, and that the whole nation not perish." ⁵¹ Now he didn't say this of himself, but being high priest that year, he prophesied that Jesus would die for the nation, ⁵² and not for the nation only, but that he might also gather together into one the children of God who are scattered abroad. ⁵³ So from that day forward they took counsel that they might put him to death. ⁵⁴ Jesus therefore walked no more openly among the Jews, but departed from there into the country near the wilderness, to a city called Ephraim. He stayed there with his disciples.

⁵⁵ Now the Passover of the Jews was at hand. Many went up from the country to Jerusalem before the Passover, to purify themselves. ⁵⁶ Then they sought for Jesus and spoke with one another as they stood in the temple, "What do you think—that he isn't coming to the feast at all?" ⁵⁷ Now the chief priests and the Pharisees had commanded that if anyone knew where he was, he should report it, that they might seize him.

12

¹ Then, six days before the Passover, Jesus came to Bethany, where Lazarus was, who had been dead, whom he raised from the dead. ² So they made him a supper there. Martha served, but Lazarus was one of those who sat at the table with him. ³ Therefore Mary took a pound of ointment of pure nard, very precious, and anointed Jesus' feet and wiped his feet with her hair. The house was filled with the fragrance of the ointment.

[4] Then Judas Iscariot, Simon's son, one of his disciples, who would betray him, said, [5] "Why wasn't this ointment sold for three hundred denarii and given to the poor?" [6] Now he said this, not because he cared for the poor, but because he was a thief, and having the money box, used to steal what was put into it.

[7] But Jesus said, "Leave her alone. She has kept this for the day of my burial. [8] For you always have the poor with you, but you don't always have me."

[9] A large crowd therefore of the Jews learned that he was there; and they came, not for Jesus' sake only, but that they might see Lazarus also, whom he had raised from the dead. [10] But the chief priests conspired to put Lazarus to death also, [11] because on account of him many of the Jews went away and believed in Jesus.

[12] On the next day a great multitude had come to the feast. When they heard that Jesus was coming to Jerusalem, [13] they took the branches of the palm trees and went out to meet him, and cried out, "Hosanna! Blessed is he who comes in the name of the Lord, the King of Israel!"

[14] Jesus, having found a young donkey, sat on it. As it is written, [15] "Don't be afraid, daughter of Zion. Behold, your King comes, sitting on a donkey's colt." [16] His disciples didn't understand these things at first, but when Jesus was glorified, then they remembered that these things were written about him, and that they had done these things to him. [17] The multitude therefore that was with him when he called Lazarus out of the tomb and raised him from the dead was testifying about it. [18] For this cause also the multitude went and met him, because they heard that he had done this sign. [19] The Pharisees therefore said among themselves, "See how you accomplish nothing. Behold, the world has gone after him."

[20] Now there were certain Greeks among those who went up to worship at the feast. [21] Therefore, these came to Philip, who

was from Bethsaida of Galilee, and asked him, saying, "Sir, we want to see Jesus." ²² Philip came and told Andrew, and in turn, Andrew came with Philip, and they told Jesus.

²³ Jesus answered them, "The time has come for the Son of Man to be glorified. ²⁴ Most certainly I tell you, unless a grain of wheat falls into the earth and dies, it remains by itself alone. But if it dies, it bears much fruit. ²⁵ He who loves his life will lose it. He who hates his life in this world will keep it to eternal life. ²⁶ If anyone serves me, let him follow me. Where I am, there my servant will also be. If anyone serves me, the Father will honor him.

²⁷ "Now my soul is troubled. What shall I say? 'Father, save me from this time'? But I came to this time for this cause. ²⁸ Father, glorify your name!"

Then a voice came out of the sky, saying, "I have both glorified it and will glorify it again."

²⁹ Therefore the multitude who stood by and heard it said that it had thundered. Others said, "An angel has spoken to him."

³⁰ Jesus answered, "This voice hasn't come for my sake, but for your sakes. ³¹ Now is the judgment of this world. Now the prince of this world will be cast out. ³² And I, if I am lifted up from the earth, will draw all people to myself." ³³ But he said this, signifying by what kind of death he should die.

³⁴ The multitude answered him, "We have heard out of the law that the Christ remains forever. How do you say, 'The Son of Man must be lifted up'? Who is this Son of Man?"

³⁵ Jesus therefore said to them, "Yet a little while the light is with you. Walk while you have the light, that darkness doesn't overtake you. He who walks in the darkness doesn't know where he is going. ³⁶ While you have the light, believe in the light, that you may become children of light." Jesus said these things, and he departed and hid himself from them. ³⁷ But though he had done so many signs before them, yet they didn't believe in him,

[38] that the word of Isaiah the prophet might be fulfilled, which he spoke:

"Lord, who has believed our report?
To whom has the arm of the Lord been revealed?"

[39] For this cause they couldn't believe, for Isaiah said again:
[40] "He has blinded their eyes and he hardened their heart,
lest they should see with their eyes,
and perceive with their heart,
and would turn,
and I would heal them."

[41] Isaiah said these things when he saw his glory, and spoke of him. [42] Nevertheless, even many of the rulers believed in him, but because of the Pharisees they didn't confess it, so that they wouldn't be put out of the synagogue, [43] for they loved men's praise more than God's praise.

[44] Jesus cried out and said, "Whoever believes in me, believes not in me, but in him who sent me. [45] He who sees me sees him who sent me. [46] I have come as a light into the world, that whoever believes in me may not remain in the darkness. [47] If anyone listens to my sayings and doesn't believe, I don't judge him. For I came not to judge the world, but to save the world. [48] He who rejects me, and doesn't receive my sayings, has one who judges him. The word that I spoke will judge him in the last day. [49] For I spoke not from myself, but the Father who sent me gave me a commandment, what I should say and what I should speak. [50] I know that his commandment is eternal life. The things therefore which I speak, even as the Father has said to me, so I speak."

13

¹ Now before the feast of the Passover, Jesus, knowing that his time had come that he would depart from this world to the Father, having loved his own who were in the world, he loved them to the end. ² During supper, the devil having already put into the heart of Judas Iscariot, Simon's son, to betray him, ³ Jesus, knowing that the Father had given all things into his hands, and that he came from God and was going to God, ⁴ arose from supper, and laid aside his outer garments. He took a towel and wrapped a towel around his waist. ⁵ Then he poured water into the basin, and began to wash the disciples' feet and to wipe them with the towel that was wrapped around him. ⁶ Then he came to Simon Peter. He said to him, "Lord, do you wash my feet?"

⁷ Jesus answered him, "You don't know what I am doing now, but you will understand later."

⁸ Peter said to him, "You will never wash my feet!"

Jesus answered him, "If I don't wash you, you have no part with me."

⁹ Simon Peter said to him, "Lord, not my feet only, but also my hands and my head!"

¹⁰ Jesus said to him, "Someone who has bathed only needs to have his feet washed, but is completely clean. You are clean, but not all of you." ¹¹ For he knew him who would betray him; therefore he said, "You are not all clean." ¹² So when he had washed their feet, put his outer garment back on, and sat down again, he said to them, "Do you know what I have done to you? ¹³ You call me, 'Teacher' and 'Lord.' You say so correctly, for so I am. ¹⁴ If I then, the Lord and the Teacher, have washed your feet, you also ought to wash one another's feet. ¹⁵ For I have given you an example, that you should also do as I have done to you. ¹⁶ Most certainly I tell you, a servant is not greater than his lord, neither is one who

is sent greater than he who sent him. [17] If you know these things, blessed are you if you do them. [18] I don't speak concerning all of you. I know whom I have chosen; but that the Scripture may be fulfilled, 'He who eats bread with me has lifted up his heel against me.' [19] From now on, I tell you before it happens, that when it happens, you may believe that I am he. [20] Most certainly I tell you, he who receives whomever I send, receives me; and he who receives me, receives him who sent me."

[21] When Jesus had said this, he was troubled in spirit, and testified, "Most certainly I tell you that one of you will betray me."

[22] The disciples looked at one another, perplexed about whom he spoke. [23] One of his disciples, whom Jesus loved, was at the table, leaning against Jesus' chest. [24] Simon Peter therefore beckoned to him, and said to him, "Tell us who it is of whom he speaks."

[25] He, leaning back, as he was, on Jesus' chest, asked him, "Lord, who is it?"

[26] Jesus therefore answered, "It is he to whom I will give this piece of bread when I have dipped it." So when he had dipped the piece of bread, he gave it to Judas, the son of Simon Iscariot. [27] After the piece of bread, then Satan entered into him.

Then Jesus said to him, "What you do, do quickly."

[28] Now nobody at the table knew why he said this to him. [29] For some thought, because Judas had the money box, that Jesus said to him, "Buy what things we need for the feast," or that he should give something to the poor. [30] Therefore having received that morsel, he went out immediately. It was night.

[31] When he had gone out, Jesus said, "Now the Son of Man has been glorified, and God has been glorified in him. [32] If God has been glorified in him, God will also glorify him in himself, and he will glorify him immediately. [33] Little children, I will be with you a little while longer. You will seek me, and as I said to the Jews, 'Where I am going, you can't come,' so now I tell you.

[34] A new commandment I give to you, that you love one another. Just as I have loved you, you also love one another. [35] By this everyone will know that you are my disciples, if you have love for one another."

[36] Simon Peter said to him, "Lord, where are you going?"

Jesus answered, "Where I am going, you can't follow now, but you will follow afterwards."

[37] Peter said to him, "Lord, why can't I follow you now? I will lay down my life for you."

[38] Jesus answered him, "Will you lay down your life for me? Most certainly I tell you, the rooster won't crow until you have denied me three times.

14

[1] "Don't let your heart be troubled. Believe in God. Believe also in me. [2] In my Father's house are many homes. If it weren't so, I would have told you. I am going to prepare a place for you. [3] If I go and prepare a place for you, I will come again and will receive you to myself; that where I am, you may be there also. [4] You know where I go, and you know the way."

[5] Thomas said to him, "Lord, we don't know where you are going. How can we know the way?"

[6] Jesus said to him, "I am the way, the truth, and the life. No one comes to the Father, except through me. [7] If you had known me, you would have known my Father also. From now on, you know him and have seen him."

[8] Philip said to him, "Lord, show us the Father, and that will be enough for us."

[9] Jesus said to him, "Have I been with you such a long time, and do you not know me, Philip? He who has seen me has seen

the Father. How do you say, 'Show us the Father'? [10] Don't you believe that I am in the Father, and the Father in me? The words that I tell you, I speak not from myself; but the Father who lives in me does his works. [11] Believe me that I am in the Father, and the Father in me; or else believe me for the very works' sake. [12] Most certainly I tell you, he who believes in me, the works that I do, he will do also; and he will do greater works than these, because I am going to my Father. [13] Whatever you will ask in my name, I will do it, that the Father may be glorified in the Son. [14] If you will ask anything in my name, I will do it. [15] If you love me, keep my commandments. [16] I will pray to the Father, and he will give you another Counselor, that he may be with you forever: [17] the Spirit of truth, whom the world can't receive, for it doesn't see him and doesn't know him. You know him, for he lives with you and will be in you. [18] I will not leave you orphans. I will come to you. [19] Yet a little while, and the world will see me no more; but you will see me. Because I live, you will live also. [20] In that day you will know that I am in my Father, and you in me, and I in you. [21] One who has my commandments and keeps them, that person is one who loves me. One who loves me will be loved by my Father, and I will love him, and will reveal myself to him."

[22] Judas (not Iscariot) said to him, "Lord, what has happened that you are about to reveal yourself to us, and not to the world?"

[23] Jesus answered him, "If a man loves me, he will keep my word. My Father will love him, and we will come to him and make our home with him. [24] He who doesn't love me doesn't keep my words. The word which you hear isn't mine, but the Father's who sent me.

[25] "I have said these things to you while still living with you. [26] But the Counselor, the Holy Spirit, whom the Father will send in my name, will teach you all things, and will remind you of all that I said to you. [27] Peace I leave with you. My peace I give

to you; not as the world gives, I give to you. Don't let your heart be troubled, neither let it be fearful. ²⁸You heard how I told you, 'I am going away, and I will come back to you.' If you loved me, you would have rejoiced because I said 'I am going to my Father;' for the Father is greater than I. ²⁹Now I have told you before it happens so that when it happens, you may believe. ³⁰I will no more speak much with you, for the prince of the world comes, and he has nothing in me. ³¹But that the world may know that I love the Father, and as the Father commanded me, even so I do. Arise, let's go from here.

15

¹ "I am the true vine, and my Father is the farmer. ²Every branch in me that doesn't bear fruit, he takes away. Every branch that bears fruit, he prunes, that it may bear more fruit. ³You are already pruned clean because of the word which I have spoken to you. ⁴Remain in me, and I in you. As the branch can't bear fruit by itself unless it remains in the vine, so neither can you, unless you remain in me. ⁵I am the vine. You are the branches. He who remains in me and I in him bears much fruit, for apart from me you can do nothing. ⁶If a man doesn't remain in me, he is thrown out as a branch and is withered; and they gather them, throw them into the fire, and they are burned. ⁷If you remain in me, and my words remain in you, you will ask whatever you desire, and it will be done for you.

⁸ "In this my Father is glorified, that you bear much fruit; and so you will be my disciples. ⁹Even as the Father has loved me, I also have loved you. Remain in my love. ¹⁰If you keep my commandments, you will remain in my love, even as I have kept my Father's commandments and remain in his love. ¹¹I have

spoken these things to you, that my joy may remain in you, and that your joy may be made full.

¹² "This is my commandment, that you love one another, even as I have loved you. ¹³ Greater love has no one than this, that someone lay down his life for his friends. ¹⁴ You are my friends if you do whatever I command you. ¹⁵ No longer do I call you servants, for the servant doesn't know what his lord does. But I have called you friends, for everything that I heard from my Father, I have made known to you. ¹⁶ You didn't choose me, but I chose you and appointed you, that you should go and bear fruit, and that your fruit should remain; that whatever you will ask of the Father in my name, he may give it to you.

¹⁷ "I command these things to you, that you may love one another. ¹⁸ If the world hates you, you know that it has hated me before it hated you. ¹⁹ If you were of the world, the world would love its own. But because you are not of the world, since I chose you out of the world, therefore the world hates you. ²⁰ Remember the word that I said to you: 'A servant is not greater than his lord.' If they persecuted me, they will also persecute you. If they kept my word, they will also keep yours. ²¹ But they will do all these things to you for my name's sake, because they don't know him who sent me. ²² If I had not come and spoken to them, they would not have had sin; but now they have no excuse for their sin. ²³ He who hates me, hates my Father also. ²⁴ If I hadn't done among them the works which no one else did, they wouldn't have had sin. But now they have seen and also hated both me and my Father. ²⁵ But this happened so that the word may be fulfilled which was written in their law, 'They hated me without a cause.'

²⁶ "When the Counselor has come, whom I will send to you from the Father, the Spirit of truth, who proceeds from the Father, he will testify about me. ²⁷ You will also testify, because you have been with me from the beginning.

16

¹ "I have said these things to you so that you wouldn't be caused to stumble. ² They will put you out of the synagogues. Yes, the time is coming that whoever kills you will think that he offers service to God. ³ They will do these things because they have not known the Father nor me. ⁴ But I have told you these things so that when the time comes, you may remember that I told you about them. I didn't tell you these things from the beginning, because I was with you. ⁵ But now I am going to him who sent me, and none of you asks me, 'Where are you going?' ⁶ But because I have told you these things, sorrow has filled your heart. ⁷ Nevertheless I tell you the truth: It is to your advantage that I go away; for if I don't go away, the Counselor won't come to you. But if I go, I will send him to you. ⁸ When he has come, he will convict the world about sin, about righteousness, and about judgment; ⁹ about sin, because they don't believe in me; ¹⁰ about righteousness, because I am going to my Father, and you won't see me any more; ¹¹ about judgment, because the prince of this world has been judged.

¹² "I still have many things to tell you, but you can't bear them now. ¹³ However, when he, the Spirit of truth, has come, he will guide you into all truth, for he will not speak from himself; but whatever he hears, he will speak. He will declare to you things that are coming. ¹⁴ He will glorify me, for he will take from what is mine and will declare it to you. ¹⁵ All things that the Father has are mine; therefore I said that he takes of mine and will declare it to you.

¹⁶ "A little while, and you will not see me. Again a little while, and you will see me."

¹⁷ Some of his disciples therefore said to one another, "What is this that he says to us, 'A little while, and you won't see me,

and again a little while, and you will see me;' and, 'Because I go to the Father'?" [18] They said therefore, "What is this that he says, 'A little while'? We don't know what he is saying."

[19] Therefore Jesus perceived that they wanted to ask him, and he said to them, "Do you inquire among yourselves concerning this, that I said, 'A little while, and you won't see me, and again a little while, and you will see me'? [20] Most certainly I tell you that you will weep and lament, but the world will rejoice. You will be sorrowful, but your sorrow will be turned into joy. [21] A woman, when she gives birth, has sorrow because her time has come. But when she has delivered the child, she doesn't remember the anguish any more, for the joy that a human being is born into the world. [22] Therefore you now have sorrow, but I will see you again, and your heart will rejoice, and no one will take your joy away from you.

[23] "In that day you will ask me no questions. Most certainly I tell you, whatever you may ask of the Father in my name, he will give it to you. [24] Until now, you have asked nothing in my name. Ask, and you will receive, that your joy may be made full.

[25] "I have spoken these things to you in figures of speech. But the time is coming when I will no more speak to you in figures of speech, but will tell you plainly about the Father. [26] In that day you will ask in my name; and I don't say to you that I will pray to the Father for you, [27] for the Father himself loves you, because you have loved me, and have believed that I came from God. [28] I came from the Father and have come into the world. Again, I leave the world and go to the Father."

[29] His disciples said to him, "Behold, now you are speaking plainly, and using no figures of speech. [30] Now we know that you know all things, and don't need for anyone to question you. By this we believe that you came from God."

[31] Jesus answered them, "Do you now believe? [32] Behold, the time is coming, yes, and has now come, that you will be scattered,

everyone to his own place, and you will leave me alone. Yet I am not alone, because the Father is with me. [33] I have told you these things, that in me you may have peace. In the world you have trouble; but cheer up! I have overcome the world."

17

[1] Jesus said these things, then lifting up his eyes to heaven, he said, "Father, the time has come. Glorify your Son, that your Son may also glorify you; [2] even as you gave him authority over all flesh, so he will give eternal life to all whom you have given him. [3] This is eternal life, that they should know you, the only true God, and him whom you sent, Jesus Christ. [4] I glorified you on the earth. I have accomplished the work which you have given me to do. [5] Now, Father, glorify me with your own self with the glory which I had with you before the world existed.

[6] "I revealed your name to the people whom you have given me out of the world. They were yours, and you have given them to me. They have kept your word. [7] Now they have known that all things whatever you have given me are from you, [8] for the words which you have given me I have given to them; and they received them, and knew for sure that I came from you. They have believed that you sent me. [9] I pray for them. I don't pray for the world, but for those whom you have given me, for they are yours. [10] All things that are mine are yours, and yours are mine, and I am glorified in them. [11] I am no more in the world, but these are in the world, and I am coming to you. Holy Father, keep them through your name which you have given me, that they may be one, even as we are. [12] While I was with them in the world, I kept them in your name. I have kept those whom you have given me. None of them is lost except the son of destruction, that the

Scripture might be fulfilled. ¹³ But now I come to you, and I say these things in the world, that they may have my joy made full in themselves. ¹⁴ I have given them your word. The world hated them because they are not of the world, even as I am not of the world. ¹⁵ I pray not that you would take them from the world, but that you would keep them from the evil one. ¹⁶ They are not of the world, even as I am not of the world. ¹⁷ Sanctify them in your truth. Your word is truth. ¹⁸ As you sent me into the world, even so I have sent them into the world. ¹⁹ For their sakes I sanctify myself, that they themselves also may be sanctified in truth.

²⁰ "Not for these only do I pray, but for those also who will believe in me through their word, ²¹ that they may all be one; even as you, Father, are in me, and I in you, that they also may be one in us; that the world may believe that you sent me. ²² The glory which you have given me, I have given to them, that they may be one, even as we are one, ²³ I in them, and you in me, that they may be perfected into one, that the world may know that you sent me and loved them, even as you loved me. ²⁴ Father, I desire that they also whom you have given me be with me where I am, that they may see my glory which you have given me, for you loved me before the foundation of the world. ²⁵ Righteous Father, the world hasn't known you, but I knew you; and these knew that you sent me. ²⁶ I made known to them your name, and will make it known; that the love with which you loved me may be in them, and I in them."

18

¹ When Jesus had spoken these words, he went out with his disciples over the brook Kidron, where there was a garden, into which he and his disciples entered. ² Now Judas, who betrayed him, also knew the place, for Jesus often met there with his

disciples. [3] Judas then, having taken a detachment of soldiers and officers from the chief priests and the Pharisees, came there with lanterns, torches, and weapons. [4] Jesus therefore, knowing all the things that were happening to him, went out and said to them, "Who are you looking for?"

[5] They answered him, "Jesus of Nazareth."

Jesus said to them, "I am he."

Judas also, who betrayed him, was standing with them. [6] When therefore he said to them, "I am he," they went backward and fell to the ground.

[7] Again therefore he asked them, "Who are you looking for?"

They said, "Jesus of Nazareth."

[8] Jesus answered, "I told you that I am he. If therefore you seek me, let these go their way," [9] that the word might be fulfilled which he spoke, "Of those whom you have given me, I have lost none."

[10] Simon Peter therefore, having a sword, drew it, struck the high priest's servant, and cut off his right ear. The servant's name was Malchus. [11] Jesus therefore said to Peter, "Put the sword into its sheath. The cup which the Father has given me, shall I not surely drink it?"

[12] So the detachment, the commanding officer, and the officers of the Jews seized Jesus and bound him, [13] and led him to Annas first, for he was father-in-law to Caiaphas, who was high priest that year. [14] Now it was Caiaphas who advised the Jews that it was expedient that one man should perish for the people.

[15] Simon Peter followed Jesus, as did another disciple. Now that disciple was known to the high priest, and entered in with Jesus into the court of the high priest; [16] but Peter was standing at the door outside. So the other disciple, who was known to the high priest, went out and spoke to her who kept the door, and brought in Peter. [17] Then the maid who kept the door said to Peter, "Are you also one of this man's disciples?"

He said, "I am not."

[18] Now the servants and the officers were standing there, having made a fire of coals, for it was cold. They were warming themselves. Peter was with them, standing and warming himself.

[19] The high priest therefore asked Jesus about his disciples and about his teaching.

[20] Jesus answered him, "I spoke openly to the world. I always taught in synagogues and in the temple, where the Jews always meet. I said nothing in secret. [21] Why do you ask me? Ask those who have heard me what I said to them. Behold, they know the things which I said."

[22] When he had said this, one of the officers standing by slapped Jesus with his hand, saying, "Do you answer the high priest like that?"

[23] Jesus answered him, "If I have spoken evil, testify of the evil; but if well, why do you beat me?"

[24] Annas sent him bound to Caiaphas, the high priest.

[25] Now Simon Peter was standing and warming himself. They said therefore to him, "You aren't also one of his disciples, are you?"

He denied it and said, "I am not."

[26] One of the servants of the high priest, being a relative of him whose ear Peter had cut off, said, "Didn't I see you in the garden with him?"

[27] Peter therefore denied it again, and immediately the rooster crowed.

[28] They led Jesus therefore from Caiaphas into the Praetorium. It was early, and they themselves didn't enter into the Praetorium, that they might not be defiled, but might eat the Passover. [29] Pilate therefore went out to them and said, "What accusation do you bring against this man?"

³⁰ They answered him, "If this man weren't an evildoer, we wouldn't have delivered him up to you."

³¹ Pilate therefore said to them, "Take him yourselves, and judge him according to your law."

Therefore the Jews said to him, "It is illegal for us to put anyone to death," ³² that the word of Jesus might be fulfilled, which he spoke, signifying by what kind of death he should die.

³³ Pilate therefore entered again into the Praetorium, called Jesus, and said to him, "Are you the King of the Jews?"

³⁴ Jesus answered him, "Do you say this by yourself, or did others tell you about me?"

³⁵ Pilate answered, "I'm not a Jew, am I? Your own nation and the chief priests delivered you to me. What have you done?"

³⁶ Jesus answered, "My Kingdom is not of this world. If my Kingdom were of this world, then my servants would fight, that I wouldn't be delivered to the Jews. But now my Kingdom is not from here."

³⁷ Pilate therefore said to him, "Are you a king then?"

Jesus answered, "You say that I am a king. For this reason I have been born, and for this reason I have come into the world, that I should testify to the truth. Everyone who is of the truth listens to my voice."

³⁸ Pilate said to him, "What is truth?"

When he had said this, he went out again to the Jews, and said to them, "I find no basis for a charge against him. ³⁹ But you have a custom that I should release someone to you at the Passover. Therefore, do you want me to release to you the King of the Jews?"

⁴⁰ Then they all shouted again, saying, "Not this man, but Barabbas!" Now Barabbas was a robber.

19

¹ So Pilate then took Jesus and flogged him. ² The soldiers twisted thorns into a crown and put it on his head, and dressed him in a purple garment. ³ They kept saying, "Hail, King of the Jews!" and they kept slapping him.

⁴ Then Pilate went out again, and said to them, "Behold, I bring him out to you, that you may know that I find no basis for a charge against him."

⁵ Jesus therefore came out, wearing the crown of thorns and the purple garment. Pilate said to them, "Behold, the man!"

⁶ When therefore the chief priests and the officers saw him, they shouted, saying, "Crucify! Crucify!"

Pilate said to them, "Take him yourselves and crucify him, for I find no basis for a charge against him."

⁷ The Jews answered him, "We have a law, and by our law he ought to die, because he made himself the Son of God."

⁸ When therefore Pilate heard this saying, he was more afraid. ⁹ He entered into the Praetorium again, and said to Jesus, "Where are you from?" But Jesus gave him no answer. ¹⁰ Pilate therefore said to him, "Aren't you speaking to me? Don't you know that I have power to release you and have power to crucify you?"

¹¹ Jesus answered, "You would have no power at all against me, unless it were given to you from above. Therefore he who delivered me to you has greater sin."

¹² At this, Pilate was seeking to release him, but the Jews cried out, saying, "If you release this man, you aren't Caesar's friend! Everyone who makes himself a king speaks against Caesar!"

¹³ When Pilate therefore heard these words, he brought Jesus out and sat down on the judgment seat at a place called "The Pavement", but in Hebrew, "Gabbatha." ¹⁴ Now it was the

Preparation Day of the Passover, at about the sixth hour. He said to the Jews, "Behold, your King!"

¹⁵ They cried out, "Away with him! Away with him! Crucify him!"

Pilate said to them, "Shall I crucify your King?"

The chief priests answered, "We have no king but Caesar!"

¹⁶ So then he delivered him to them to be crucified. So they took Jesus and led him away. ¹⁷ He went out, bearing his cross, to the place called "The Place of a Skull", which is called in Hebrew, "Golgotha", ¹⁸ where they crucified him, and with him two others, on either side one, and Jesus in the middle. ¹⁹ Pilate wrote a title also, and put it on the cross. There was written, "JESUS OF NAZARETH, THE KING OF THE JEWS." ²⁰ Therefore many of the Jews read this title, for the place where Jesus was crucified was near the city; and it was written in Hebrew, in Latin, and in Greek. ²¹ The chief priests of the Jews therefore said to Pilate, "Don't write, 'The King of the Jews,' but, 'he said, "I am King of the Jews."'"

²² Pilate answered, "What I have written, I have written."

²³ Then the soldiers, when they had crucified Jesus, took his garments and made four parts, to every soldier a part; and also the tunic. Now the tunic was without seam, woven from the top throughout. ²⁴ Then they said to one another, "Let's not tear it, but cast lots for it to decide whose it will be," that the Scripture might be fulfilled, which says,

"They parted my garments among them.

They cast lots for my clothing."

Therefore the soldiers did these things.

²⁵ But standing by Jesus' cross were his mother, his mother's sister, Mary the wife of Clopas, and Mary Magdalene. ²⁶ Therefore when Jesus saw his mother, and the disciple whom he loved standing there, he said to his mother, "Woman, behold, your

son!" [27] Then he said to the disciple, "Behold, your mother!" From that hour, the disciple took her to his own home.

[28] After this, Jesus, seeing that all things were now finished, that the Scripture might be fulfilled, said, "I am thirsty!" [29] Now a vessel full of vinegar was set there; so they put a sponge full of the vinegar on hyssop, and held it at his mouth. [30] When Jesus therefore had received the vinegar, he said, "It is finished!" Then he bowed his head and gave up his spirit.

[31] Therefore the Jews, because it was the Preparation Day, so that the bodies wouldn't remain on the cross on the Sabbath (for that Sabbath was a special one), asked of Pilate that their legs might be broken and that they might be taken away. [32] Therefore the soldiers came and broke the legs of the first and of the other who was crucified with him; [33] but when they came to Jesus and saw that he was already dead, they didn't break his legs. [34] However, one of the soldiers pierced his side with a spear, and immediately blood and water came out. [35] He who has seen has testified, and his testimony is true. He knows that he tells the truth, that you may believe. [36] For these things happened that the Scripture might be fulfilled, "A bone of him will not be broken." [37] Again another Scripture says, "They will look on him whom they pierced."

[38] After these things, Joseph of Arimathaea, being a disciple of Jesus, but secretly for fear of the Jews, asked of Pilate that he might take away Jesus' body. Pilate gave him permission. He came therefore and took away his body. [39] Nicodemus, who at first came to Jesus by night, also came bringing a mixture of myrrh and aloes, about a hundred Roman pounds. [40] So they took Jesus' body, and bound it in linen cloths with the spices, as the custom of the Jews is to bury. [41] Now in the place where he was crucified there was a garden. In the garden was a new tomb in which no man had ever yet been laid. [42] Then, because of the Jews' Preparation Day (for the tomb was near at hand), they laid Jesus there.

20

¹ Now on the first day of the week, Mary Magdalene went early, while it was still dark, to the tomb, and saw that the stone had been taken away from the tomb. ² Therefore she ran and came to Simon Peter and to the other disciple whom Jesus loved, and said to them, "They have taken away the Lord out of the tomb, and we don't know where they have laid him!"

³ Therefore Peter and the other disciple went out, and they went toward the tomb. ⁴ They both ran together. The other disciple outran Peter and came to the tomb first. ⁵ Stooping and looking in, he saw the linen cloths lying there; yet he didn't enter in. ⁶ Then Simon Peter came, following him, and entered into the tomb. He saw the linen cloths lying, ⁷ and the cloth that had been on his head, not lying with the linen cloths, but rolled up in a place by itself. ⁸ So then the other disciple who came first to the tomb also entered in, and he saw and believed. ⁹ For as yet they didn't know the Scripture, that he must rise from the dead. ¹⁰ So the disciples went away again to their own homes.

¹¹ But Mary was standing outside at the tomb weeping. So as she wept, she stooped and looked into the tomb, ¹² and she saw two angels in white sitting, one at the head and one at the feet, where the body of Jesus had lain. ¹³ They asked her, "Woman, why are you weeping?"

She said to them, "Because they have taken away my Lord, and I don't know where they have laid him." ¹⁴ When she had said this, she turned around and saw Jesus standing, and didn't know that it was Jesus.

¹⁵ Jesus said to her, "Woman, why are you weeping? Who are you looking for?"

She, supposing him to be the gardener, said to him, "Sir, if you have carried him away, tell me where you have laid him, and I will take him away."

¹⁶ Jesus said to her, "Mary."

She turned and said to him, "Rabboni!" which is to say, "Teacher!"†

¹⁷ Jesus said to her, "Don't hold me, for I haven't yet ascended to my Father; but go to my brothers and tell them, 'I am ascending to my Father and your Father, to my God and your God.' "

¹⁸ Mary Magdalene came and told the disciples that she had seen the Lord, and that he had said these things to her. ¹⁹ When therefore it was evening on that day, the first day of the week, and when the doors were locked where the disciples were assembled, for fear of the Jews, Jesus came and stood in the middle and said to them, "Peace be to you."

²⁰ When he had said this, he showed them his hands and his side. The disciples therefore were glad when they saw the Lord. ²¹ Jesus therefore said to them again, "Peace be to you. As the Father has sent me, even so I send you." ²² When he had said this, he breathed on them, and said to them, "Receive the Holy Spirit! ²³ If you forgive anyone's sins, they have been forgiven them. If you retain anyone's sins, they have been retained."

²⁴ But Thomas, one of the twelve, called Didymus, wasn't with them when Jesus came. ²⁵ The other disciples therefore said to him, "We have seen the Lord!"

But he said to them, "Unless I see in his hands the print of the nails, put my finger into the print of the nails, and put my hand into his side, I will not believe."

²⁶ After eight days, again his disciples were inside and Thomas was with them. Jesus came, the doors being locked, and stood in the middle, and said, "Peace be to you." ²⁷ Then he said to Thomas, "Reach here your finger, and see my hands. Reach

here your hand, and put it into my side. Don't be unbelieving, but believing."

²⁸ Thomas answered him, "My Lord and my God!"

²⁹ Jesus said to him, "Because you have seen me, you have believed. Blessed are those who have not seen and have believed."

³⁰ Therefore Jesus did many other signs in the presence of his disciples, which are not written in this book; ³¹ but these are written that you may believe that Jesus is the Christ, the Son of God, and that believing you may have life in his name.

21

¹ After these things, Jesus revealed himself again to the disciples at the sea of Tiberias. He revealed himself this way. ² Simon Peter, Thomas called Didymus, Nathanael of Cana in Galilee, and the sons of Zebedee, and two others of his disciples were together. ³ Simon Peter said to them, "I'm going fishing."

They told him, "We are also coming with you." They immediately went out and entered into the boat. That night, they caught nothing. ⁴ But when day had already come, Jesus stood on the beach; yet the disciples didn't know that it was Jesus. ⁵ Jesus therefore said to them, "Children, have you anything to eat?"

They answered him, "No."

⁶ He said to them, "Cast the net on the right side of the boat, and you will find some."

They cast it therefore, and now they weren't able to draw it in for the multitude of fish. ⁷ That disciple therefore whom Jesus loved said to Peter, "It's the Lord!"

So when Simon Peter heard that it was the Lord, he wrapped his coat around himself (for he was naked), and threw himself into the sea. ⁸ But the other disciples came in the little boat (for they were not far from the land, but about two hundred cubits away), dragging the net full of fish. ⁹ So when they got out on the land, they saw a fire of coals there, with fish and bread laid on it. ¹⁰ Jesus said to them, "Bring some of the fish which you have just caught."

¹¹ Simon Peter went up, and drew the net to land, full of one hundred fifty-three great fish. Even though there were so many, the net wasn't torn.

¹² Jesus said to them, "Come and eat breakfast!"

None of the disciples dared inquire of him, "Who are you?" knowing that it was the Lord.

¹³ Then Jesus came and took the bread, gave it to them, and the fish likewise. ¹⁴ This is now the third time that Jesus was revealed to his disciples after he had risen from the dead. ¹⁵ So when they had eaten their breakfast, Jesus said to Simon Peter, "Simon, son of Jonah, do you love me more than these?"

He said to him, "Yes, Lord; you know that I have affection for you."

He said to him, "Feed my lambs." ¹⁶ He said to him again a second time, "Simon, son of Jonah, do you love me?"

He said to him, "Yes, Lord; you know that I have affection for you."

He said to him, "Tend my sheep." ¹⁷ He said to him the third time, "Simon, son of Jonah, do you have affection for me?"

Peter was grieved because he asked him the third time, "Do you have affection for me?" He said to him, "Lord, you know everything. You know that I have affection for you."

Jesus said to him, "Feed my sheep. ¹⁸ Most certainly I tell you, when you were young, you dressed yourself and walked where you wanted to. But when you are old, you will stretch out your hands, and another will dress you and carry you where you don't want to go."

[19] Now he said this, signifying by what kind of death he would glorify God. When he had said this, he said to him, "Follow me."

[20] Then Peter, turning around, saw a disciple following. This was the disciple whom Jesus loved, the one who had also leaned on Jesus' chest at the supper and asked, "Lord, who is going to betray you?" [21] Peter, seeing him, said to Jesus, "Lord, what about this man?"

[22] Jesus said to him, "If I desire that he stay until I come, what is that to you? You follow me." [23] This saying therefore went out among the brothers that this disciple wouldn't die. Yet Jesus didn't say to him that he wouldn't die, but, "If I desire that he stay until I come, what is that to you?"

[24] This is the disciple who testifies about these things, and wrote these things. We know that his witness is true. [25] There are also many other things which Jesus did, which if they would all be written, I suppose that even the world itself wouldn't have room for the books that would be written.